Amelia Edith Huddleston Barr

A Rose of a Hundred Leaves

A Love Story

Amelia Edith Huddleston Barr

A Rose of a Hundred Leaves
A Love Story

ISBN/EAN: 9783744685191

Printed in Europe, USA, Canada, Australia, Japan

Cover: Foto ©Thomas Meinert / pixelio.de

More available books at **www.hansebooks.com**

A ROSE

OF A

HUNDRED LEAVES

A Love-Story

BY

AMELIA E. BARR

AUTHOR OF "FRIEND OLIVIA," "THE BOW OF ORANGE
RIBBON," "JAN VEDDER'S WIFE," ETC.

NEW YORK
DODD, MEAD AND COMPANY
1891

University Press:
JOHN WILSON AND SON, CAMBRIDGE.

CONTENTS.

———

A ROSE OF A HUNDRED LEAVES.

CHAPTER I.

THE WILD ROSE IS THE SWEETEST.

I TELL again the oldest and the newest story of all the world, — the story of Invincible Love!

This tale divine — ancient as the beginning of things, fresh and young as the passing hour — has forms and names various as humanity. The story of Aspatria Anneys is but

one of these, — one leaf from all the roses
in the world, one note of all its myriad
of songs.

Aspatria was born at Scat-Ambar, an
old house in Allerdale. It had Skiddaw
to shelter it on the northwest; and it
looked boldly out across the Solway, and
into that sequestered valley in Furness
known as "the Vale of the Deadly
Nightshade." The plant still grew there
abundantly, and the villagers still kept
the knowledge of its medical value taught
them by the old monks of Furness. For
these curious, patient herbalists had discovered the blessing hidden in the fair,
poisonous amaryllis, long before modern
physicians called it "belladonna."

The plant, with all its lovely relations,
had settled in the garden at Scat-Ambar.
Aspatria's mother had loved them all:
the girl could still remember her thin
white hands clasping the golden jonquils
in her coffin. This memory was in her
heart, as she hastened through the lonely
place one evening in spring. It ought to

have been a pleasant spot, for it was full
of snowdrops and daffodils, and many
sweet old-fashioned shrubs and flowers;
but it was a stormy night, and the blos-
soms were plashed and downcast, and all
the birds in hiding from the fierce wind
and driving rain.

She was glad to get out of the gray,
wet, shivery atmosphere, and to come into
the large hall, ruddy and glowing with fire
and candle-light. Her brothers William
and Brune sat at the table Will was
counting money; it stood in small gold
and silver pillars before him. Brune was
making fishing-flies. Both looked up at
her entrance; they did not think words
necessary for such a little maid. Yet
both loved her; she was their only sister,
and both gave her the respect to which
she was entitled as co-heir with them of
the Ambar estate.

She was just sixteen, and not yet beautiful. She was too young for beauty. Her
form was not developed; she would prob-
ably gain two or three inches in height;

and her face, though exquisitely modelled,
wanted the refining which comes either
from a multitude of complex emotions or
is given at once by some great heart-
sorrow. Yet she had fascination for those
capable of feeling her charm. Her large
brown eyes had their childlike clearness;
they looked every one in the face with its
security of good-will. Her mouth was a
tempting mouth; the lips had not lost
their bow-shape; they were red and pouting, but withal ever ready to part. She
might have been born with a smile. Her
hair, soft and dark, had that rarest quality
of soft hair, — a tendency to make itself into little curls and tendrils and stray down
the white throat and over the white brow;
yet it was carefully parted and confined
in two long braids, tied at the ends with
a black ribbon.

She wore a black dress. It was plainly
made, and its broad ruffle around the open
throat gave it an air of simplicity almost
childlike in effect. Her arms below the
elbows were uncovered, and her hands

were small and finely formed, as patrician hands should be. There was no ring upon them, and no bracelet above them. She wore neither brooch nor locket, nor ornament of any kind about her person; only a daffodil laid against the snowy skin of her bosom. Even this effect was not the result of coquetry; it was a holy and loving sentiment materialized.

Altogether, she was a girl quite in keeping with the antique, homelike air of the handsome room she entered; her look, her manner, and even her speech had the local stamp; she was evidently a daughter of the land. Her brothers resembled her after their masculine fashion. They were big men, whom nature had built for the spaces of the moors and mountains and the wide entrances of these old Cumberland homes. They would have been pushed to pass through narrow city doorways. A fine open-air colour was in their faces; they had that confident manner which great physical strength imparts, and that air of conscious pride which is born in lords of the soil.

Indeed, William and Brune Anneys made one understand how truthfully pop·ular nomenclature has called an Englishman " John Bull." For whoever has seen a bull in its native pastures — proud, obstinate, conscious of his strength, and withal a little surly — must understand that there is a taurine basis to the English character, finely expressed by the national appellation.

A great thing was to happen that hour, and all three were as unconscious of the approaching fate as if it was to be a part of another existence. Squire William finished his accounts, and played a game of chess with his brother. Aspatria walked up and down the hall, with her hands clasped behind her, or sat still in the Squire's hearth-chair, with her dress lifted a little in front, to let the pleasant heat fall upon her ankles. She did not think of reading or of sewing, or of improving the time in any way. Perhaps she was not as dependent on books as the women of this generation. Aspatria's mind was sensitive and observing; it lived very well on its own ideas.

The storm increased in violence; the rain beat against the windows, and the wind howled at the nail-studded oak door, as if it intended to blow it down. A big ploughman entered the room, shyly pulled his front hair, and looked with stolid inquiry into his master's face. The Squire pushed aside the chess-board, rose, and went to the hearth-stone; for he was young in his authority, and he felt himself on the hearth-stone to hold an impregnable position.

" Well, Steve Bell, what is it? "

" Be I to sow the high land next, sir? "

" If you can have a face or back wind, it will be best; if you have an elbow-wind, you must give the land an extra half-bushel."

" Be I to sow mother-of-corn [1] on the east holme? "

" It is matterless. Is it going to be a flashy spring? "

[1] Clover.

"A right season, sir,— plenty of manger-meat."

"How is the weather?"

"The rain is near past ; it will take up at midnight."

As he spoke, Aspatria, who had been sitting with folded hands and half-shut eyes, straightened herself suddenly, and threw up her head to listen. There was certainly the tramp of a horse's feet, and in a moment the door was loudly and impatiently struck with the metal handle of a riding-whip.

Steve Bell went to

answer the summons; Brune trailed slowly
after him. Aspatria and the Squire heard
nothing on the hearth but a human voice
blown about and away by the wind. But
Steve's reply was distinct enough, —

" You be wanting Redware Hall, sir?
Cush! it's unsensible to try for it. The
hills are slape as ice ; the becks are full ;
the moss will make a mouthful of you —
horse and man — to-night."

The Squire went forward, and Aspatria
also. Aspatria lifted a candle, and carried
it high in her hand. That was the first
glimpse of her that Sir Ulfar Fenwick
had.

"You must stay at Seat-Ambar to-
night," said William Anneys. "You cannot go farther and be sure of your life.
You are welcome here heartily, sir."

The traveller dismounted, gave his horse
to Steve, and with words of gratitude
came out of the rain and darkness into the
light and comfort of the home opened to
him. "I am Ulfar Fenwick," he said, —
" Fenwick of Fenwick and Outerby ; and

I think you must be William Anneys of Ambar-Side."

"The same, sir. This is my brother Brune, and my sister Aspatria. You are dreeping wet, sir. Come to my room and change your clothing."

Sir Ulfar bowed and smiled assent; and the bow and the smile were Aspatria's. Her cheeks burned; a strange new life was in all her veins. She hurried the housekeeper and the servants, and she brought out the silver and the damask, and the famous crystal cup in its stand of gold, which was the lucky bowl of Ambar-Side. When Fenwick came back to the hall, there was a feast spread for him; and he ate and drank, and charmed every one with his fine manner and his witty conversation.

They sat until midnight, — an hour strange to Seat-Ambar. No one native in that house had ever seen it before, no one ever felt its mysterious influence. Sir Ulfar had been charming them with tales of the strange lands he had visited, and the

strange peoples who dwelt in them. He
had not spoken much to Aspatria, but it
was in her face he had found inspiration
and sympathy. For her young eyes
looked out with such eager interest, with
glances so seeking, so without guile and
misgiving, that their bright rays found a
corner in his heart into which no woman
had ever before penetrated. And she was
equally subjugated by his more modern
orbs, — orbs with that steely point of brilliant light, generated by large experience
and varied emotion, — electric orbs, such
as never shone in the elder world.

When the clock struck twelve, Squire
Anneys rose with amazement. " Why, it
is strike of midnight! " he said " It is
past all, how the hours have flown! But
we must n't put off sleeping-time any
longer. Good-night heartily to you, sir.
It will be many a long day till I forget this
night. What doings you have seen, sir! "

He was talking thus to his guest, as he
led him to the guest-room. Aspatria still
stood by the dying fire. Brune rose

silently, stretched his big arms, and said:
"I'll be going likewise.   You had best
remember the time of
night, Aspatria."

"What do you think
of him, Brune?"

"Fenwick! I would n't
think too high of him.
One might have to come
down a peg or two. He
sets a good deal of store by
himself, I should say."

"You and I are of two ways
of judging, Brune."

"Never mind; time will let
light into all our ways of
judging."

He went yawning upstairs and
Aspatria slowly followed. She was not
a bit sleepy. She was wider awake
than she had ever been before. Her
hands quivered like a swallow's wings;
her face was rosy and luminous. She
removed her clothing, and unbraided her
hair and shook it loose over her slim,

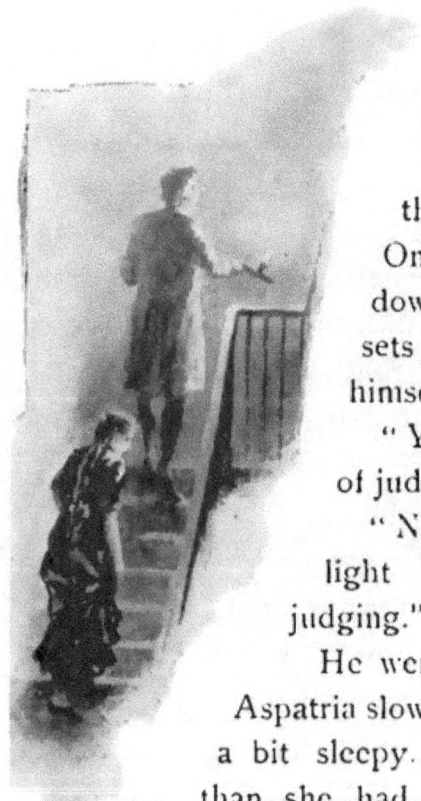

shoulders. There was a smile on her lips through all these preparations for sleep, — a smile innocent and glad. Suddenly she lifted the candle and carried it to the mirror. She desired to look at herself, and she blushed deeply as she gratified the wish. Was she fair enough to please this wonderful stranger?

It was the first time such a query had ever come to her heart. She was inclined to answer it honestly. Holding the light slightly above her head, she examined her claims to his regard. Her expressive face, her starry eyes, her crimson, pouting lips, her long dark hair, her slight, virginal figure in its gown of white muslin scantily trimmed with English thread-lace, her small, bare feet, her air of childlike, curious happiness, — all these things, taken together, pleased and satisfied her desires, though she knew not how or why.

Then she composed herself with intentional earnestness. She must "say her prayers." As yet it was only saying prayers with Aspatria, — only a holy habit. A

large Book of Common Prayer stood open
against an oaken rest on a table; a cushion
of black velvet was beneath it. Ere she
knelt, she reflected that it was very late,
and that her Collect and Lord's Prayer
would be sufficient. Youth has such confidence in the sympathy of God. She
dropped softly on her knees and said her
portion. God would understand the rest.
The little ceremony soothed her, as a
mother's kiss might have done; and with
a happy sigh she put out the light. The
old house was dark and still, but her
guardian angel saw her small hands loose
lying on the snowy linen, and heard her
whisper, " Dear God! how happy I am ! "
And this joyous orison was the acceptable
prayer that left the smile of peace upon
her sleeping face.

In the guest-chamber Ulfar Fenwick
was also holding a session with himself.
He had come to his room very wide
awake; midnight was an early hour to
him. And the incidents he had been telling filled his mind with images of the past.

He could not at once put them aside.
Women he had loved and left visited his
memory,—light loves of a season, in which
both had declared themselves broken-
hearted at parting, and both had known
that they would very soon forget. Neither
was much to blame: the maid had long
ceased to remember his vows and kisses;
he, in some cases, had forgotten her name.
Yet, sitting there by the glowing oak logs,
he had visions of fair faces in all kinds of
surroundings, — in lighted halls, in moon-
lit groves under the great stars of the
tropics, on the Shetland seas when the
aurora made for lovers an enchanted atmosphere and a light in which beauty was
glorified. Well, they had passed as April
passes, and now, —

> As a glimpse of a burnt-out ember
> Recalls a regret of the sun,
> He remembered, forgot, and remembered
> What love saw done and undone.

Aspatria was different from all. He
whispered her strange name on his lips,
and he thought it must have wandered

from some sunny southern clime into these
northern solitudes. His eyes shone; his
heart beat. He said to it: "Make room
for this innocent little one! What a darling she is! How clear, how candid, how
beautiful! Oh, to be loved by such a
woman! Oh, to kiss her!—to feel her
kiss me!" He set his mouth tightly; the
soft dreamy look in his face changed to
one of purpose and pleasure.

"I shall win her, or die for it," he said.
"By Saint George! I would rather die than
know that any other man had married her."

Yet the thought of marriage somewhat
sobered him. "I should have to give up
my voyage to the Spanish Colonies,—and
I am very much interested in their struggle.
I could not take her to Mexico, I suppose,
—there is nothing but fighting there;
and I could not—no, I could not leave
her. If she were mine, I should hate to
have any one else breathe the same air with
her. I could not endure that others should
speak to her. I should want to strike any
man who touched her hand. Perhaps I

had better go away in the morning, and
ride this road no more. I have made my
plans."

And fate had made other plans. Who
can fight against his destiny? When he
saw Aspatria in the morning, every plan
that did not include her seemed unworthy
of his consideration. She was ten times
lovelier in the daylight. She had that
fresh invincible charm which women of
culture and intellect seldom have: she
was inspired by her heart. It taught her
a thousand delightful subjugating ways.
She served his breakfast with her own fair
hands; she offered him the first sweet
flowers in the garden; she fluttered around
his necessities, his desires, his intentions,
with a grace and a kindness nothing but
love could have taught her.

He thanked her with marvellous glances,
with smiles, with single words dropped
only for her ears, with all the potent elo-
quence which passion and experience
teach. And he had to pay the price, as
all men must do. The lesson he taught

he also learned. "Aspatria!" he
said, in soft, penetrating accents;
and when she answered his

call and
came to his side,
her dress trailing
across his feet be-
witched him.   They
were in the garden,
and he clasped her
hand, and went down
the budding alleys
with her, speechless, but gazing
into her face until she dropped
her tremulous, transparent lids before her eyes; they were too full of
light and love to show to any mortal.

   The sky was white and blue, the air

fresh and sweet; the swallows had just come, and were chattering with the starlings; hundreds of daffodils " danced in the wind" and lighted the ground at their feet; troops of celandines starred the brook that babbled by the bee-skips; the southernwood, the wall-flower, the budding thyme and sweet-brier, — a thousand exhalations filled the air and intensified that intoxication of heart and senses which makes the first stage of love's fever delirious.

Fenwick went away in the afternoon, and his adieus were mostly made to the Squire. He had done his best to win his favour, and he had been successful. He left Seat-Ambar under an engagement to return soon and try his skill in wrestling and pole-leaping with Brune. Aspatria knew he would return: a voice which Fenwick's voice only echoed told her so.. She watched him from her own window across the meadows, and up the mountain, until he was lost to her vision.

She was doubtless very much in love,

though as yet she had not admitted the
fact to herself. The experience had come
with a really shocking swiftness. Her
heart was half angry and half abashed by
its instantaneous surrender. Two circumstances had promoted this condition.
First, the singular charm of the man.
Ulfar Fenwick was unlike any one she had
ever seen. The squires and gentlemen
who came to Seat-Ambar were physically
the finest fellows in England, but noble
women look for something more than
mere bulk in a man. Sir Ulfar Fenwick
had this something more. Culture, travel,
great experience with women, had added to
his heroic form a charm flesh and sinew
alone could never compass. And if he had
lacked all other physical advantages, he
possessed eyes which had been filled to
the brim with experiences of every kind,
— gray eyes with pure, full lids thickly
fringed, — eyes always lustrous, sometimes
piercingly bright. Secondly, Aspatria had
no knowledge which helped her to ward
off attack or protract surrender. In a

multitude of lovers there is safety; but Fenwick was Aspatria's first lover.

He rode hard, as if he would ride from fate. Perhaps he hoped at this early stage of feeling to do as he had often done before, —

To love — and then ride away.

He had also a fresh, pressing anxiety to see his sister, who was Lady of Redware Manor. Seven years — and much besides

years — had passed since they met. She
was his only sister, and ten years his
senior. She loved him as mothers love,
unquestioningly, with miraculous excuses
for all his shortcomings. She had been
watching for his arrival many hours before
he appeared.

"Ulfar! how welcome you are!" she
cried, with tears in her eyes and her voice.
"Oh, my dear! how happy I am to see
you once more!"

She might have been his only love, he
kissed and embraced and kissed her again
so fondly. Oh, wondrous tie of blood
and kinship! At that moment there really
seemed to Ulfar Fenwick no one in the
whole world half so dear as his sister
Elizabeth.

He told her he had lost his way in the
storm and been detained by Squire Anneys; and she praised the Squire, and
said that she would evermore love him
for his kindness. "I met him once, at
the Election Ball in Kendal. He danced
with me; 'we neighbour each other,' you

see; and they are a grand old family, I
can tell you."

"There is a younger brother, called
Brune."

"I never saw him."

"A sister also, — a child yet, but very
handsome. You ought to see her."

"Why?"

"You would like her. I do."

"Ulfar, there is a 'thus far' in everything. In your wooing and pursuing,
the line lies south of Seat-Ambar. To
wrong a woman of that house would be
wicked and dangerous."

"Why should I wrong her? I have no
intention to do so. I say she is a lovely
lady, a great beauty, worthy of honest
love and supreme devotion."

"Such a rant about love and beauty!
Nine tenths of the men who talk in this
way do but blaspheme Love by taking his
name in vain."

"However, Elizabeth, it is marriage or
the Spanish colonies for me. It is Miss
Anneys, or Cuba, New Orleans, and

Mexico. Santa Anna is a supreme villain; I have a fancy to see such a specimen."

"You are then between the devil and the deep sea; and I should say that the one-legged Spaniard was preferable to the deep sea of matrimony."

" She is so fair! She has a virgin timidity that enchants me."

" It will become matronly indecision, or mental weakness of will. In the future it will drive you frantic."

" Her sweet sensibility — "

" Will crystallize into passionate irritation or callous opposition. These child-like, tender, clinging maidens are often capable of sudden and dangerous action. Better go to Cuba, or even to Mexico, Ulfar."

"I suppose she has wealth. You will admit that excellence? "

" She is co-heir with her brothers. She may have two thousand pounds a year. You cannot afford to marry a girl so poor."

" I have not yet come to regard a large

sum of money as a kind of virtue, or the want of it as a crime."

"Your wife ought to represent you. How can this country-girl help you in the society to which you belong?"

"Society! What is society? In its elemental verity it means toil, weariness, loss of rest and health, useless expense, envy, disappointment, heart-burnings, — all for the sake of exchanging entertainments with A and B, C and D. It means chaff instead of wheat."

"If you want to be happy, Ulfar, put this girl out of your mind. I am sure her brothers will oppose your suit. They will not let their sister leave Allerdale. No Anneys has ever done so."

"You have strengthened my fancy, Elizabeth. There is a deal of happiness in the idea of prevailing, of getting the mastery, of putting hindrances out of the way."

"Well, I have given you good advice."

"There are many 'counsels of perfection' nobody dreams of following. To advise a man in love not to love, is one of them."

"Love!" she cried scornfully. "Before you make such a fuss about the Spanish Colonies and their new-found freedom, free yourself, Ulfar! You have been a slave to some woman all your life. You are one of those men who are naturally not their own property. A child can turn you hither and thither; a simple country girl can lead you."

He laughed softly, and murmured, —

"There is a rose of a hundred leaves,
But the wild rose is the sweetest."

CHAPTER II.

FORGIVE ME, CHRIST!

THE ultimatum reached by Fenwick in the consideration of any subject was, to please himself. In the case of Aspatria Anneys he was particularly determined to do so. It was in vain Lady Redware entreated him to be rational. How could he be rational? It was the preponderance of the emotional over the rational in his nature which imparted so strong a personality to him. He grasped all circumstances by feeling rather than by reason.

In a few days he was again at Seat-Ambar. Aspatria drew him, as the candle draws the moth which has once burned its wings at it. And among the simple Anneys folk he found a hearty welcome. With Squire William he travelled the hills, and counted the flocks, and speculated on the value of the iron-ore cropping out of the ground. With Brune he went line-fishing, and in the wide barns tried his skill in wrestling or pole-leaping or single-stick. He tolerated the rusticity of the life, for the charming moments he found with Aspatria.

No one like Ulfar Fenwick had ever visited Ambar-Side. To the young men, who read nothing but the Gentleman's Magazine and the Whitehaven Herald, and to Aspatria, who had but a volume of the Ladies' Garden Manual, Notable Things, her Bible and Common Prayer, Fenwick was a book of travel, song, and story, of strange adventures, of odd bits of knowledge, and funny experiences. Things old and new fell from his handsome lips. Squire William and Brune heard them with grave attention, with delight and laughter; Aspatria with eyes full of wonder and admiration.

As the season advanced and they grew more familiar, Aspatria was thrown naturally into his society. The Squire was in the hay-field; Brune had his task there also. Or they were down at the Long Pool, washing the sheep, or on the fells, shearing them. In the haymaking, Aspa-

tria and Fenwick made some pretence of assistance ; but they both very soon wearied of the real labour. Aspatria would toss a few furrows of the warm, sweet grass; but it was much sweeter to sit down under the oak-tree with Fenwick at her side, and watch the moving picture, and listen to the women singing in their high shrill voices, as they turned the

swaths, the Song of the Mower, and the
men mournfully shouting out the chorus
to it, —

   " We be all like grass!   We be all like grass! "

As for the oak, it liked them to sit under
it; all its leaves talked to each other about
them.   The starlings, though they are
always in a hurry, stopped to look at the
lovers, and went off with a Q-q-q of satisfaction.   The crows, who are a bad lot,
croaked innuendoes, and said it was to be
hoped that evil would not come of such
folly.   But Aspatria and Fenwick listened
only to each other; they saw the whole
round world in each other's eyes.

Fenwick spoke very low; Aspatria had
to droop her ear to his mouth to understand his words.   And they were such
delightful words, she could not bear to
lose one of them.   Then, as the sun grew
warm, and the scent of the grass filled the
soft air, and the haymakers were more and
more subdued and quiet, heavenly lan-
guors stole over them.   They sat hand in

hand, — Aspatria sometimes with shut eyes
humming to herself, sometimes dreamily
pulling the long grass at her side; Fenwick mostly silent, yet often whispering
those words which are single because they
are too sweet to be double, — "Darling!
Dearest! Angel!" and the words drew
her eyes to his eyes, drew her lips to his
lips; ere she was aware, her heart had
passed from her in long, loving, stolen
kisses. On the fells, in the garden, in
the empty, silent rooms of the old house,
it was a repetition of the same divine
song, with wondrously celestial variations.
Goethe puts in Faust an Interlude in
Heaven: Fenwick and Aspatria were in
their Interlude.

One evening they stood among the
wheat-sheaves. The round, yellow har-
vest-moon was just rising above the fells,
and the stars trembling into vision. The
reapers had gone away; their voices made
faint, fitful echoes down the misty lane.
The Squire was driving home one load of
ripe wheat, and Brune another. Aspatria

said softly, " The day is over. We must
go home. Come!"

She stood in the warm mystical light,
with one hand upon the bound sheaf, the
other stretched out to him.   Her slim
form in its white dress, her upturned face,
her star-like eyes,—he saw all at a glance.
He was subjugated to the innermost room
of his heart.   He answered, with inexpres-
sible emotion, —

"Come! Come to me, my Dear One!
My Love! My Joy! My Wife!"   He
held her close to his heart ; he claimed
her by no formal special yes, but by all
the sweet reluctances and sweeter yield-
ings, the thousand nameless consents won
day by day.

Oh, the glory of that homeward walk!
The moon beamed upon them.   The trees
bent down to touch them.   The heath
and the honeysuckle made a posy for
them. The nightingale sang them a can-
ticle. They did not seem to walk ; they
trod on ether; they moved as people
move in happy dreams of other stars,

where thought and wish are motion. It
would have been heaven upon earth if
those minutes could have lasted; but it
was only an interlude.

That night Fenwick spoke to Squire
William and asked him for his sister. The
Squire was honestly confounded by the
question. Aspatria was such a little lass!
It was beyond everything to talk of marrying her. Still, in his heart he was proud
and pleased at such high fortune for the
little lass; and he said, as soon as Fenwick's father and family came forward as
they should do, he would never be the one
to say nay.

Fenwick's father lived at Fenwick Castle, on the shore of bleak Northumberland. He was an old man, but his natural
feelings and wisdom were not abated. He
consulted the History of Cumberland, and
found that the family of Ambar-Anneys
was as ancient and honourable as his own.
But the girl was country-bred, and her
fortune was small, and in a measure dependent upon her brother's management

of the estate. A careless
master of Ambar-Side
would make Aspa-
tria poor. While
he was consid-
ering these
things, Lady
Redware ar-
rived at the
castle, and they talked
over the matter together.

"I expected Ulfar to marry very
differently, and I must say I am disappointed. But I suppose it will be useless
to make any opposition, Elizabeth," the
old man said to his daughter.

" Quite useless, father. But absence
works miracles. Try to secure
twelve months. You ought
to go to a warm climate
this winter; ask Ulfar
to take you to Italy.
In a year time may
re-shuffle the cards.
And you must write to the

girl, and to her eldest brother, who is a
fine fellow and as proud as Lucifer. I
called upon them before I left Cumberland. She is very handsome."

"Handsome! Old men know, Elizabeth, that six months after a man is married, it makes little difference to him
whether his wife is handsome or not."

"That may be, or it may not be, father.
The thing to consider is, that young men
unfortunately persist in marrying for that
first six months."

"Well, then, fortune pilots many a ship
not steered. Suppose we leave things to
circumstances?"

"No, no! Human affairs are for the
most part arranged in such a way that
those turn out best to which most care
is devoted."

So the letters were thoughtfully written;
the one to Aspatria being of a paternal
character, that to her brother polite and
complimentary. To his son Ulfar the old
baronet made a very clever appeal. He
reminded him of his great age, and of the

few opportunities left for showing his affection and obedience. He regretted the necessity for a residence in Italy during the winter, but trusted to his son's love to see him through the experience. He congratulated Ulfar on winning the love of a young girl so fresh and unspoiled by the world, but kindly insisted upon the wisdom of a little delay, and the great benefit this delay would be to himself.

It was altogether a very temperate, wise letter, appealing to the best side of Ulfar's nature. Squire William read it also, and gave it his most emphatic approval. He was in no hurry to lose his little sister. She was but a child yet, and knew nothing of the world she was going into; and "surely to goodness," he said, looking at the child, "she will have a lot of things to look after, before she can think of wedding."

This last conjecture touched Aspatria on a very womanly point. Of course there were all her "things" to get ready. She had never possessed more than a few

frocks at a time, and those of the simplest
character; but she was quite alive to the
necessity of an elaborate wardrobe, and
she had also an instinctive sense of what
would be proper for her position.

So the suggestions of Ulfar's father were
accepted in their entirety, and the old
gentleman was put into a very good temper by the fact. And what was a year?
" It will pass like a dream," said Ulfar.
" And I shall write constantly to you, and
you will write to me; and when we meet
again it will be to part no more." Oh,
the poverty of words in such straits as
these! Men say the same things in the
same extremities now that have been said
millions of times before them. And Aspatria felt as if there ought to have been
entirely new words, to express the joy of
their betrothal and the sorrow of their
parting.

The short delay of a last week together
was perhaps a mistake. A very young
girl, to whom great joy and great sorrow
are alike fresh experiences, may afford a

prolonged luxury of the emotions of parting. Love, more worldly-wise, deprecates
its demonstrativeness, and would avert it
altogether. The farewell walks, the sentimental souvenirs, the pretty and petty devices of love's first dream, are tiresome to
more practised lovers; and Ulfar had often
proved what very cobwebs they were to
bind a straying fancy.

"Absence makes the heart grow fonder."
Perhaps so, if the last memory be an altogether charming one. It was, unfortunately, not so in Aspatria's case. It should
have been a closely personal farewell with
Ulfar alone; but Squire Anneys, in his
hospitable ignorance, gave it a public character. Several neighbouring squires and
dames came to breakfast. There was cup-
drinking, and toasting, and speech-making;
and Ulfar's last glimpse of his betrothed
was of her standing in the wide porch, surrounded by a waving, jubilant crowd of
strangers, whose intermeddling in his joy
he deeply resented. Anneys had invited
them in accord with the traditions of his

house and order. Fenwick thought it was
a device to make stronger his engagement
to Aspatria.

"As if it needed such contrivances!"
he muttered angrily. "When it does, it is
a broken thread, and no Anneys can knot
it again."

The weeks that followed were full of
new interests to Aspatria. Mistress Frostham, the wife of a near shepherd-lord, had
been the friend of Aspatria's mother; she
was fairly conversant with the world outside the fells and dales, and she took the
girl under her care, accompanied her to
Whitehaven, and directed her in the purchase of all considered necessary for the
wife of Ulfar Fenwick.

Then the deep snows shut in Scat-
Ambar, and the great white hills stood
round about it like fortifications. But as
often as it was possible the Dalton postman fought his way up there, with his
packet of accumulated mail; for he knew
that a warm welcome and a large reward
awaited him. In the main, the long same

days went happily by. William and Brune
had a score of resources for the season ; the farm-servants worked in the
barn ; they were making and mending
sacks for the wheat, and caps
for the sheeps' heads
in fly-time,
sharpening
scythes and
tools, doing the in-
door work of a
great farm, and

mostly singing as they
did it.

As Aspatria sat in her room,
surrounded by fine cambric and
linen and that exquisite English
thread-lace now gone out of fashion, she

could hear their laughter and their song,
and she unconsciously set her stitches to
its march and melody. The days were
not long to her. So many dozens of garments to make with her own slight fingers! She had not a moment to waste,
but the necessity was one of the sweetest
delight. The solitude and secrecy of her
labour added to its charm. She never
took her sewing into the parlour. And yet
she might have done so: William and
Brune had a delicacy of affection for her
which would have made them blind to her
occupation and densely stupid as to its
design.

So, although the days were mostly alike,
they were not unhappily so; and at intervals destiny sent her the surprises she
loved. One morning in the beginning of
February, Aspatria felt that the postman
ought to come; her heart presaged him.
The day was clear and warm, — so much
so, that the men working in the barn had
all the windows open. They were singing
in rousing tones the famous North Country

song to the barley-mow, and drinking it
through all its verses, out of the jolly
brown bowl, the nipperkin, the quarter-
pint, the quart and the pottle,—the gallon
and the anker,—the hogshead and the
pipe,—the well, and the river, and the
ocean,—and then rolling back the chorus,
from ocean to the jolly brown bowl. Suddenly, while a dozen men were shouting in
unison,—

" Here 's a health to the barley mow ! "

the verse was broken by the cry of " Here
comes Ringham the postman ! " Then
Aspatria ran to the window and saw him
climbing the fell. She did not like to go
downstairs until Will called her; but she
could not sew another stitch. And when
at last the aching silence in her ears was
filled by Will's joyful " Come here, Aspatria ! Here is such a parcel as never
was,—from foreign parts too ! " she hardly
knew how her feet twinkled down the long
corridor and stairs.

The parcel was from Rome. Ulfar had

sent it to his London banker, and the banker had sent a special messenger to Dalton with it. Over the fells at that season no one but Ringham could have found a safe way; and Ringham was made so welcome that he was quite imperious. He ordered himself a rasher of bacon, and a bowl of the famous barley broth, and spread himself comfortably before the great hearth-place. At the table stood Aspatria, William, and Brune. Aspatria was nervously trying to undo the seals and cords that bound love's message to her. Will finally took his pocket-knife and cut them. There was a long letter, and a box containing exquisite ornaments of Roman cameos, — precious onyx, made more precious by work of rare artistic beauty, a comb for her dark hair, a necklace for her white throat, bracelets for her slender wrists, a girdle of stones linked with gold for her waist. Oh, how full of simple delight she was! She was too happy to speak. Then Will discovered a smaller package. It was for himself and Brune.

Will's present was a cameo ring, on which
were engraved the Anneys and Fenwick
arms. Brune had a scarf-pin, representing
a lovely Hebe. It was a great day at
Seat-Ambar. Aspatria could work no
more; Will and Brune felt it impossible
to finish the game they had begun.

There is a tide in everything: this was
the spring-tide of Aspatria's love. In its
overflowing she was happy for many a
day after her brothers had begun to spec-
ulate and wonder why Ringham did not
come. Suddenly it struck her that the
snow was gone, and the road open, and
that there was no letter. She began to
worry, and Will quietly rode over to Dalton, to ask if any letter was lying there.
He came back empty-handed, silent, and
a little surly. The anniversary of their
meeting was at hand: surely Ulfar would
remember it, so Aspatria thought, and she
watched from dawn to dark, but no token
of remembrance came. The flowers began
to bloom, the birds to sing, the May sunshine flooded the earth with glory, but

fear and doubt and dismay and daily disappointment made deepest, darkest winter
in the low, long room where Aspatria
watched and waited.   Her sewing had
been thrown aside.   The half-finished garments, neatly folded, lay under a cover
she had no strength to remove.

In June she wrote a pitiful little note to
her lover.   She said that he ought to tell
her, if he was tired of their engagement.
She told Will what she had said, and asked
him to post the letter.   He answered
angrily, "Don't you write a word to him,
good or bad!"   And he tore the letter
into twenty pieces before her eyes.

"Oh, Will, I cannot bear it!"

"Thou art a woman: bear what other
women have tholed before thee."   Then
he went angrily from her presence.   Brune
was thrumming on the window-pane.   She
thought he looked sorry for her; she
touched his arm and said, "Brune, will
you take a letter to Dalton post for
me?"

"For sure I will.   Go thy ways and

write it, and I'll be gone before Will is back."

It was an unfortunate letter, as letters written in a hurry always are. Absolute silence would have piqued and worried Ulfar. He would have fancied her ill, dying perhaps; and the uncertainty, vague and portentous, would have prompted him to action, if only to satisfy his own mind. Sometimes he feared that a girl so sensitive would fade away in neglect; and he expected a letter from William Anneys saying so. But a hurried, halting, not very correct epistle, whose whole tenour was, "What is the matter? What have I done? Do you remember last year at this time?" irritated him beyond reply.

He was still in Italy when it reached him. Sir Thomas Fenwick was not likely ever to return to England. He was slowly dying, and he had been removed to a villa in the Italian hills. And Elizabeth Redware had a friend with her, a young widow just come from Athens, who affected at times its splendid picturesque national costume. She was a very bright, handsome woman, whose fine education had been supplemented by travel, society, and a rather unhappy matrimonial experience. She knew how to pique and provoke, how to flirt to the very edge of danger and then sheer off, how to manipulate men before the fire of passion, as witches used to manipulate their waxen images before the blazing coals.

She had easily won Ulfar's confidence; she had even assisted in the selection of the cameos; and she declared to Elizabeth that she would not for a whole world interfere between Ulfar and his pretty innocent! A natural woman was such a phenomenon! She was glad Ulfar was going to marry a phenomenon.

Elizabeth knew her better. She gave the couple opportunity, and they needed nothing more. There were already between them a good understanding, transparent secrets, little jokes, a confessed confidence. They quickly became affectionate. The lovely Sarah, relict of Herbert Sandys,

Esq., not only reminded Ulfar of his vows
to Aspatria, but in the very reminder she
tempted him to break them. When Aspatria's letter was put into his hand, she

was with him, marvellously arrayed in
tissue of silver and brilliant colours. A
head-dress of gold coins glittered in her
fair braided hair; her long white arms
were shining with bracelets; she was at

once languid and impulsive, provoking Elizabeth and Ulfar to conversation, and then amazing them by the audacity and contradiction of her opinions.

" It is so fortunate," she said, " that Ulfar has found a little out-of-the-way girl to appreciate his great beauty. The world at present does not think much of masculine beauty. A handsome fellow who starts for any of its prizes is judged to be frivolous and poetical, perhaps immoral: you see Byron's beauty made him unfit for a legislator, he could do nothing but write poetry. I should say it was Ulfar's best card to marry this innocent with the queer name: with his face and figure, he will never get into Parliament. No one would trust him with taxes. He is born to make love, and he and his country Phyllis can go simpering and kissing through life together. If I were interested in Ulfar — "

" You are interested in Ulfar, Sarah," interrupted Elizabeth. " You said so to me last night."

" Did I? Nevertheless, life does not

give us time really to question ourselves, and it is the infirmity of my nature to mistake feeling for evidence."

" You must not change your opinions so quickly, Sarah."

" It is often an element of success to change your opinions. It is hesitating among a variety of views that is fatal. The man who does not know what he wants is the man who is held cheap."

" I am sure I know what I want, Sarah." And as he spoke, Ulfar looked with intelligence at the fair widow, and in answer she shot from her bright blue eyes a bolt of summer lightning that set aflame at once the emotional side of Ulfar's nature.

" You say strange things, Sarah. I wish it was possible to understand you."

" ' Who shall read the interpretation thereof? ' is written on everything we see, especially on women."

" I believe," said Elizabeth, " that Ulfar has quarrelled with his country maid. Is there a quarrel, Ulfar, really? "

" No," he answered, with some temper.

Sarah nodded at Ulfar, and said softly: "The absent must be satisfied with the second place. However, if you have quarrelled with her, Ulfar, turn over a new leaf. I found that out when poor Sandys was alive. People who have to live together must blot a leaf now and then with their little tempers. The only thing is to turn over a new one."

"If anything unpleasant happens to me," said Ulfar, "I try to bury it."

"You cannot do it. The past is a ghost not to be laid; and a past which is buried alive, it is terrible." It was Sarah who spoke, and with a sombre earnestness not in keeping with her usual character. There was a minute's pregnant silence, and it was broken by the entrance of a servant with a letter. He gave it to Ulfar.

It was Aspatria's sorrowful, questioning note. Written while Brune waited, it was badly written, incorrectly constructed and spelled, and generally untidy. It had the same effect upon Ulfar that a badly dressed, untidy woman would have had.

He was ashamed of the irregular, childish scrawl. He did not take the trouble to put himself in the atmosphere in which the anxious, sorrowful words had been written. He crushed the paper in his hand with much the same contemptuous temper with which Elizabeth had seen him treat a dunning letter. She knew, however, that this letter was from Aspatria, and, saying something about her father, she went into an adjoining room, and left Ulfar and Sarah together. She thought Sarah would be the proper alterative.

The first words Sir Thomas Fenwick uttered regarded Aspatria. Turning his head feebly, he asked: "Has Ulfar quarrelled with Miss Anneys? I hear nothing of her lately."

"I think he is tired of his fancy for her. There is no quarrel."

"She was a good girl, — eh? Kindhearted, beautiful, — eh, Elizabeth?"

"She certainly was."

He said no more then; but at midnight, when Ulfar was sitting beside him, he

called his son, and spoke to him on the
subject. " I am going — almost gone —
the way of all flesh, Ulfar. Take heed of
my last words. You promised to make
Miss Anneys your wife, — eh?"

" I did, father."

" Do not break your promise. If she
gives it back to you, that might be well;
but you cannot escape from your own
word and deed. Honour keeps the door of
the house of life. To break your word is
to set the door wide open, — open for
sorrow and evil of all kinds. Take care,
Ulfar."

The next day he died, and one of Ulfar's
first thoughts was that the death set him
free from his promise for one year at the
least. A year contained a multitude of
chances. He could afford to write to
Aspatria under such circumstances. So
he answered her letter at once, and it
seemed proper to be affectionate, prepara-
tory to reminding her that their marriage
was impossible until the mourning for Sir
Thomas was over. Also death had soft-

ened his heart, and his father's last words had made him indeterminate and a little superstitious. A clever woman of the world would not have believed in this letter; its *aura* — subtle but persistent, as the perfume of the paper — would have made her doubt its fondest lines. But Aspatria had no idea other than that certain words represented absolutely certain feelings.

The letter made her joyful. It brought back the roses to her cheeks, the spring of motion to her steps. She began to work in her room once more. Now and then her brothers heard her singing the old song she had sung so constantly with Ulfar, —

> " A shepherd in a shade his plaining made,
>   Of love, and lovers' wrong,
>   Unto the fairest lass that trod on grass,
>   And thus began his song :
>   ' Restore, restore my heart again,
>   Which thy sweet looks have slain,
>   Lest that, enforced by your disdain, I sing,
>   Fye ! fye on love ! It is a foolish thing !
>
> " ' Since love and fortune will, I honour still
>   Your dark and shining eye ;

What conquest will it be, sweet nymph, to thee,
   If I for sorrow die?
Restore, restore my heart again,
Which thy sweet looks have slain,
Lest that, enforced by your disdain, I sing,
Fye! fye on love! It is a foolish thing!''

But the lifting of the sorrow was only
that it might press more heavily. No
more letters came; no message of any
kind; none of the pretty love-gages he
delighted in giving during the first months
of their acquaintance. A gloom more
wretched than that of death or sickness
settled in the old rooms of Scat-Ambar.
William and Brune carried its shadow on
their broad, rosy faces into the hay-fields
and the wheat-fields. It darkened all the
summer days, and dulled all the usual
mirth-making of the ingathering feasts.
William was cross and taciturn. He loved
his sister with all his heart, but he did not
know how to sympathize with her. Even
mother-love, when in great anxiety, sometimes wraps itself in this unreasonable
irritability. Brune understood better. He
had suffered from a love-change himself;

he knew its ache and longing, its black despairs and still more cruel hopes. He was always on the lookout for Aspatria; and one day he heard news which he

thought would interest her. Lady Redware was at the Hall. William had heard it a week before, but he had not considered it prudent to name the fact. Brune had a kinder intelligence.

"Aspatria," he said, "Redware Hall is open again. I saw Lady Redware in the village."

"Brune! Oh, Brune, is he there too?"

5

" No, he is n't. . I made sure of that."

"Brune, I want to go to Redware.
Perhaps his sister may tell me the truth.
Go with me. Oh, Brune, go with me! I
am dying of suspense and uncertainty."

" Ay, they 're fit to kill anybody, let
alone a little lass like you. It will put
William about, and it may make bad
bread between us; but I 'll go with you,
even if we do have a falling out. I 'm not
flayed for William's rages."

The next market-day Brune kept his
word. As soon as Squire Anneys had
climbed the fell breast and passed over
the brow of the hill, Brune was at the door
with horses for Aspatria and himself. She
was a good rider, and they made the distance, in spite of hills and hollows, in two
hours. Lady Redware was troubled at the
visit, but she came to the door to welcome
Aspatria, and she asked Brune with particular warmth to come into the house with
his sister. Brune knew better; he was
sure in such a case that it would prove a
mere formal call, and that Aspatria would

never have the courage to ask the questions she wished to.

But Aspatria had come to that point of mental suffering when she wanted to know the truth, even though the truth was the worst. Lady Redware saw the determination on her face, and resolved to gratify it. She was shocked at the change in Aspatria's appearance. Her beauty was, in a measure, gone. Her eyes were hollow, and the lids dark and swollen with weeping. Her figure was more angular. The dew of youth, the joy of youth, was over. She drooped like a fading flower. If Ulfar saw her in such condition he might pity, but assuredly he would not admire her.

Lady Redware kissed the poor girl. "Come in, my dear," she said kindly. "How ill you look! Here is wine: take a drink."

"I am ill. I even hope I am dying. Life is so hard to bear. Ulfar has forgotten me. I have vexed him, and cannot find out in what way. If you would only tell me!"

"You have not vexed him at all."

"What then?"

"He is tired, or he has seen a fresher face. That is Ulfar's great fault. He loves too well, because he does not love very long. Can you not forget him?"

"No."

"You must have other lovers?"

"No. I never had a lover until Ulfar wooed me. I will have none after him. I shall love him until I die."

"What folly!"

"Perhaps. I am only a foolish child. If I had been wise and clever, he would not have left me. It is my fault. Do you believe he will ever come to Seat-Ambar again?"

"I do not think he will. It is best to tell you the truth. My dear, I am truly sorry for you! Indeed I am, Aspatria!"

The girl had covered her face with her thin white hands. Her attitude was so hopeless that it brought the tears to Lady Redware's eyes. Hoping to divert her attention, she said, —

" Who called you Aspatria?"

" It was my mother's name. She was born in Aspatria, and she loved the place very much."

" Where is it, child? I never heard of it."

" Not far away, on the sea-coast, — a little town that brother Will says has been asleep for centuries. Such a pretty place, straggling up the hillside, and looking over the sea. Mother was born there, and she is buried there, in the churchyard. It is such an old church, one thousand years old! Mother said it was built by Saint Kentigern. I went there to pray last week, by mother's grave. I thought she might hear me, and help me to bear the suffering."

" You poor child! It is shameful of Ulfar!"

" He is not to blame. Will told me that it was a poor woman who could n't keep what she had won."

" It was very brutal in Will to say such a thing."

"He did not mean it unkindly. We are plain-spoken people, Lady Redware. Tell me, as plainly as Will would tell me, if there is any hope for me. Does Ulfar love me at all now?"

"I fear not."

"Are you sure?"

"I am sure."

"Thank you. Now I will go." She put out her hands before her, as if she was blind and had to feel her way; and in answer to all Lady Redware's entreaties to remain, to rest, to eat something, she only shook her head, and stumbled forward. Brune saw her coming. He was standing by the horses, but he left them, and went to meet his sister. Her misery was so visible that he put her in the saddle with fear. But she gathered the reins silently, and motioned him to proceed; and Aspatria's last sad smile haunted Lady Redware for many a day. Long afterward she recalled it with a sharp gasp of pity and annoyance. It was such a proud, sorrowful farewell.

She reached home, but it took the last

remnant of her strength. She was carried
to her bed, and she remained there many
weeks. The hills were white with snow,
and the winter winds were sounding among
them like the chant of a high mass, when
she came down once more to the parlor.
Even then Will carried her like a baby in
his arms. He had carried her mother in
the same way, when she began to die; and
his heart trembled and smote him. He
was very tender with his little sister, but
tempests of rage tossed him to and fro
when he thought of Ulfar Fenwick.

And he was compelled lately to think of
him very often. All over the fell-side, all
through Allerdale, it had begun to be
whispered, " Aspatria Anneys has been
deserted by her lover." How the fact had
become known it was difficult to discover:
it was as if it had flown from roof to roof
with the sparrows. Will could see it in the
faces of his neighbours, could hear it in
the tones of their speech, could feel it in
the clasp of their hands. And he thought
of these things, until he could not eat a

meal or sleep an hour in peace. His heart was on fire with suppressed rage. He told Brune that all he wanted was to lay Fenwick across his knees and break his neck. And then he spread out his mighty hands, and clasped and unclasped them with a silent force that had terrible anticipation in it. And he noticed that after her illness his sister no longer wore the circlet of diamonds which had been her betrothal-ring. She had evidently lost all hope. Then it was time for him to interfere.

Aspatria feared it when he came to her room one morning and kissed her and bade her good-by. He said he was going a bit off, and might be a week away, — happen more. But she did not dare to question him. Will at times had masterful ways, which no one dared to question.

Brune knew where his brother was going. The night before he had taken Brune to the little room which was called the Squire's room. In it there was a large oak chest, black with age and heavy with iron bars. It contained the title-deeds, and many other valuable papers. Will explained these and the other business of the farm to Brune; and Brune did not need to ask him why. He was well aware what business William Anneys was bent on, before Will said, —

"I am going to Fenwick Castle, Brune. I am going to make that measureless villain marry Aspatria."

"Is it worth while, Will?"

"It is worth while. He shall keep his promise. If he does not, I will kill him, or he must kill me."

"If he kills you, Will, he must then fight me." And Brune's face grew red and hot, and his eyes flashed angry fire.

"That is as it should be; only keep your anger at interest until you have lads to take your place. We must n't leave Ambar-Side without an Anneys to heir it. I fancy your wrath won't get cold while it is waiting."

"It will get hotter and hotter."

"And whatever happens, don't you be saving of kind words to Aspatria. The little lass has suffered more than a bit; and she is that like mother! I could n't bide, even if I was in my grave, to think of her wanting kindness."

The next morning Will went away. Brune would not talk to Aspatria about the journey. This course was a mistake; it would have done her good to talk continually of it. As it was, she was left to chew over and over the cud of her mournful anticipations. She had no womanly friend near her. Mrs. Frostham had drawn back a little when people began to talk of "poor Miss Anneys." She had daughters, and she did not feel that her friendship for the dead included the living, when the living were unfortunate and had questionable things said about them.

And the last bitter drop in Aspatria's cup full of sorrow was the hardness of her heart toward Heaven. She could not care about God; she thought God did not care for her. She had tried to make herself pray, even by going to her mother's grave, but she felt no spark of that hidden fire which is the only acceptable prayer. There was a Christ cut out of ivory, nailed to a large ebony cross, in her room. It had been taken from the grave of an old abbot in Aspatria Church, and had been in her mother's family three hundred years. It was a Christ that had been in the grave and had come back to earth. Her mother's eyes had closed forever while fixed upon it, and to Aspatria it had always been an object of supreme reverence and love. She was shocked to find herself unmoved by its white pathos. Even at her best hours she could only stand with clasped hands and streaming eyes before it, and with sad imploration cry, —

"I cannot pray! I cannot pray! Forgive me, Christ!"

CHAPTER III.

ONLY BROTHER WILL.

It was a dull raw day in late autumn, especially dull and raw near the sea, where there was an evil-looking sky to the eastward. Ulfar Fenwick stood at a window in Castle Fenwick which commanded the black, white-frilled surges. He was watching anxiously the point at which the pale gray wall of fog was thickest, a wall of inconceivable height, resting on the sea, reaching to the clouds, when suddenly there emerged from it a beautifully built schooner-yacht.

She cut her way through the mysterious barrier as if she had been a knife, and came forward with short, stubborn plunges.

All over the North Sea there are desolate places full of the cries of parting souls, but nowhere more desolate spaces than around Fenwick Castle; and as the winter was approaching, Ulfar was anxious to escape its loneliness. His yacht had been taking in supplies; she was making for the pier at the foot of Fenwick Cliff, and he was dressed for the voyage and about to start upon it. He was going to the Mediterranean, to Civita Vecchia, and his purpose was the filial one of bringing home the remains of the late baronet. He had promised faithfully to see them laid with those of his fore-elders on the windy Northumberland coast; and he felt that this duty must be done, ere he could comfortably travel the westward route he had so long desired.

He was slowly buttoning his pilot-coat, when he heard a heavy step upon the flagged passage. Many such steps had

been up and down it that hour, but none
with the same fateful sound. He turned
his face anxiously to the door, and as he
did so, it was flung open, as if by an angry
man, and William Anneys walked in,
frowning and handling his big walking-
stick with a subdued passion that filled
the room as if it had been suddenly
charged with electricity. The two men
looked steadily at each other, neither of
them flinching, neither of them betraying
by the movement of an eyelash the emotion
that sent the blood to their faces and the
wrath to their eyes.

"William Anneys! What do you
want?"

"I want you to set your wedding-day.
It must not be later than the fifteenth of
this month."

"Suppose I refuse to do so? I am going to Italy for my father's body."

"You shall not leave England until you
marry my sister."

"Suppose I refuse to do so?"

"Then you will have to take your

chances of life or death. You will give me satisfaction first; and if you escape the fate you well deserve, Brune may have better fortune."

"Duelling is now murder, sir, unless we pass over to France."

"I will not go to France. Wrestling is not murder, and we both know there is a 'throw' to kill; and I will 'throw' until I do kill, — or am killed. There's Brune after me."

"I have ceased to love your sister. I dare say she has forgotten me. Why do you insist on our marriage? Is it that she may be Lady Fenwick?"

"Look you, sir! I care nothing for lordships or ladyships; such things are matterless to me. But your desertion has set wicked suspicions loose about Miss Anneys; and the woman they dare to think her, you shall make your wife. By God in heaven, I swear it!"

"They have said wrong of Miss Anneys! Impossible!"

"No, sir! they have not said wrong.

If any man in Allerdale had dared to say
wrong, I had torn his tongue from his
mouth before I came here; and as for the
women, they know well I would hold their
husbands or brothers or sons responsible
for every ill word they spoke. But they
think wrong, and they make me feel it
everywhere. They look it, they shy off
from Aspatria,—oh, you know well enough
the kind of thing going on."

"A wrong thought of Miss Anneys is
atrocious. The angels are not more pure."
He said the words softly, as if to himself;
and William Anneys stood watching him
with an impatience that in a moment or
two found vent in an emphatic stamp with
his foot.

"I have no time to waste, sir. Are
you afraid to sup the ill broth you have
brewed?"

"Afraid!"

"I see you have no mind to marry.
Well, then, we will fight! I like that
better."

"I will fight both you and your brother,

6

make any engagement you wish; but if the fair name of Miss Anneys is in danger, I have a prior engagement to marry her. I will keep it first. Afterward I am at your service, Squire, yours and your brother's; for I tell you plainly that I shall leave my wife at the church door and never see her again."

"I care not how soon you leave her; the sooner the better. Will the eleventh of this month suit you?"

"Make it the fifteenth. To what church will you bring my fair bride?"

"Keep your scoffing for a fitter time. If you look in that way again, I will strike the smile off your lips with a hand that will leave you little smiling in the future." And he passed his walking-stick to his left, and doubled his large right hand with an ominous readiness.

"We may even quarrel like gentlemen, Mr. Anneys."

"Then don't you laugh like a black-guard, that's all."

"Answer me civilly. At what church

shall I meet Miss Anneys, and at what
hour on the fifteenth?"

"At Aspatria Church, at eleven o'clock."

"Aspatria?"

"Ay, to be sure! There will be wit-
nesses there, I can tell you, — generations
of them, centuries of generations. They
will see that you do the right thing, or
they will dog your steps till you have paid
the uttermost farthing of the wrong. Mind
what you do, then!"

"The dead frighten me no more than
the living do."

"You will find out, maybe, what the
vengeance of the dead is. I would be
willing to leave you to it, if you shab off,
and I am not sure but you will."

"William Anneys, you are sure I will
not. You are saying such things to provoke me to a fight."

"What reason have I to be sure? All
the vows you made to Aspatria you have
counted as a fool's babble."

"I give you my word of honour. Between gentlemen that is enough."

"To be sure, to be sure! Gentlemen can make it enough. But a poor little lass, what can she do but pine herself into a grave?"

"I will listen to you no longer, Squire Anneys. If your sister's good name is at stake, it is my first duty to shield it with my own name. If that does not satisfy your sense of honour, I will give you and your brother whatever satisfaction you desire. On the fifteenth of this month, at eleven o'clock, I will meet you at Aspatria Church. Where shall I find the place?"

"It is not far from Gosforth and Dalton, on the coast. You cannot miss it, unless you never look for it."

"Sir!"

"Unless you never look for it. I do not feel to trust you. But this is a promise made to a man, made to William Anneys; and he will see that you keep it, or else that you pay for the breaking of it."

"Good-morning, Squire. There is no necessity to prolong such an unpleasant visit."

" Nay, I will not 'good-morning' with
you. I have not a good wish of any kind
for you."

With these defiant words he left the
castle, and Fenwick threw off his pilot-
coat and sat
down to con-
sider. First
thoughts gen-
erally come
from the sel-
fish, and there-
fore the worst, side
of any nature; and
Fenwick's first thoughts
were that his yacht was ready to sail,
and that he could go away, and stay away
until Aspatria married, or some other
favourable change took place. He cared
little for England. With good management he could bring home and bury his
father's dust without the knowledge of
William Anneys. Then there was the
west! America was before him, north and
south. He had always promised himself

to see the whole western continent ere he
settled for life in England.

Such thoughts were naturally foremost,
but he did not encourage them. He felt
no lingering sentiment of pity or love for
Aspatria, but he realized very clearly what
suspicion, what the slant eye, the whispered word, the scornful glance, the doubt-
ful shrug, meant in those primitive valleys.
And he had loved the girl dearly ; he had
promised to marry her. If she wished him
to keep his promise, if it was a necessity to
her honour, then he would redeem with his
own honour his foolish words. He told
himself constantly that he had not a particle
of fear, that he despised Will and Brune
Anneys and their brutal vows of vengeance ; but — but perhaps they did unconsciously influence him. Life was sweet
to Ulfar Fenwick, full of new dreams and
hopes set in all kinds of new surroundings.
For Aspatria Anneys why should he die?
It was better to marry her. The girl had
been sweet to him, very sweet ! After all,
he was not sure but he preferred that she

should be so bound to him as to prevent
her marrying any other man. He still
liked her well enough to feel pleasure in
the thought that he had put her out of the
reach of any future lover she might have.

Squire Anneys rode home in what
Brune called " a pretty temper for any
man." His horse was at the last point of
endurance when he reached Seat-Ambar,
he himself wet and muddy, " cross and
unreasonable beyond everything." Aspatria feared the very sound of his voice.
She fled to her room and bolted the door.
At that hour she felt as if death would be
the best thing for her; she had brought
only sorrow and trouble and apprehended
disgrace to all who loved her.

" I think God has forgotten me too!"
she cried, glancing with eyes full of an-
guish to the pale Crucified One hanging
alone and forsaken in the darkest corner
of the room. Only the white figure was
visible; the cross had become a part of
the shadows. She remembered the joyous, innocent prayers that had been wont

to make peace in her heart and music on her lips; and she looked with a sorrow that was almost reproach at her Book of Common Prayer, lying dusty and neglected on its velvet cushion. In her rebellious, hopeless grief, she had missed all its wells of comfort. Oh, if an angel would only open her eyes! One had come to Hagar in the desert: Aspatria was almost in equal despair.

Yet when she heard her brother Will's voice she knew not of any other sanctuary than the little table which held her Bible and Prayer Book, and upon which the wan, sad ivory Christ looked down. In speechless misery, with clasped hands and low-bowed head, she knelt there. Will's voice, strenuous and stern, reached her at intervals. She knew from the silence in the kitchen and farm-offices, and the hasty movements of the servants, that Will was cross; and she greatly feared her eldest brother when he was in what Brune called one of his rages.

A long lull was followed by a sharp call.

It was Will calling her name. She felt it
impossible to answer, impossible to move;
and as he ascended the stairs and came

grumbling along the corridor, she crouched lower and lower. He was at her door, his hand on the latch; then a few piteous words broke from her lips: "Help, Christ, Saviour of the world!"

Instantly, like a flash of lightning, came the answer, "It is I. Be not afraid." She said the words herself, gave to her heart the promise and the comfort of it, and, so saying them, she drew back the bolt and stood facing her brother. He had a candle in his hand, and it showed her his red, angry face, and showed him the pale, resolute countenance of a woman who had prayed and been comforted.

He walked into the room and put the candle down on a small table in its centre. They both stood a moment by it; then Aspatria lifted her face to her brother and kissed him. He was taken aback and softened, and troubled at his heart. Her suffering was so evident; she was such a gray shadow of her former self.

"Aspatria! Aspatria! my little lass!" Then he stopped and looked at her again.

"What is it, Will? Dear Will, what is
it?"

"You must be married on the fifteenth.
Get something ready. I will see Mrs.
Frostham and ask her to help you a bit."

"Whom am I to marry, Will? On the
fifteenth? It is impossible! See how ill
I am!"

"You are to marry Ulfar Fenwick. Ill?
Of course you are ill; but you must go to
Aspatria Church on the fifteenth. Ulfar
Fenwick will meet you there. He will
make you his wife."

"You have forced him to marry me. I
will not go, I will not go. I will not
marry Ulfar Fenwick."

"You shall go, if I carry you in my
arms! You shall marry him, or I — will
— kill — you!"

"Then kill me! Death does not terrify
me. Nothing can be more cruel hard than
the life I have lived for a long time."

He looked at her steadily, and she
returned the gaze. His face was like a
flame; hers was white as snow.

"There are things in life worse than death, Aspatria. There is dishonour, disgrace, shame."

"Is sorrow dishonour? Is it a disgrace to love? Is it a shame to weep when love is dead?"

"Ay, my little lass, it may be a great wrong to love and to weep. There is a shadow around you, Aspatria; if people speak of you they drop their voices and shake their heads; they wonder, and they think evil. Your good name is being smiled and shaken away, and I cannot find any one, man or woman, to thrash for it."

She stood listening to him with wide-open eyes, and lips dropping a little apart, every particle of colour fled from them.

"It is for this reason Fenwick is to marry you."

"You forced him; I know you forced him." She seemed to drag the words from her mouth; they almost shivered; they broke in two as they fell halting on the ear.

"Well, I must say he did not need forcing, when he heard your good name was in danger. He said, manly enough, that he would make it good with his own name. I do not much think I could have either frightened or flogged him into marrying you."

"Oh, Will! I cannot marry him in this way! Let people say wicked things of me, if they will."

"Nay, I will not! I cannot help them thinking evil; but they shall not look it, and they shall not say it."

"Perhaps they do not even think it, Will. How can you tell?"

"Well enough, Aspatria. How many women come to Ambar-Side now? If you gave a dance next week, you could not get a girl in Allerdale to accept your invitation."

"Will!"

"It is the truth. You must stop all this by marrying Ulfar Fenwick. He saw it was only just and right: I will say that much for him."

" Let me alone until morning.   I will
do what you say. — Oh, mother ! mother !
I want mother now !"

" My poor little lass ! I am only brother
Will ; but I am sorry for thee, I am that ! "

She tottered to the
bedside, and he lifted her
gently, and laid her on it; and then, as
softly as if he was afraid of waking her, he
went out of the room.   Outside the door
he found Brune.   He had taken off his
shoes, and was in his stocking-feet.   Will
grasped him by the shoulder and led him
to his own chamber.

"What were you watching me for? What were you listening to me for? I have a mind to hit you, Brune."

"You had better not hit me, Will. I was not bothering myself about you. I was watching Aspatria. I was listening, because I knew the madman in you had got loose, and I was feared for my sister. I was not going to let you say or do things you would be sorry to death for when you came to yourself. And so you are going to let that villain marry Aspatria? You are not of my mind, Will. I would not let him put a foot into our decent family, or have a claim of any kind on our sister."

"I have done what I thought best."

"I don't say it is best."

"And I don't ask for your opinion. Go to your own room, Brune, and mind your own affairs."

And Brune, brought up in the religious belief of the natural supremacy of the elder brother, went off without another word, but with a heart full to overflowing of turbulent, angry thoughts.

In the morning Will went to see Mrs.
Frostham. He told her of his interview
with Ulfar Fenwick, and begged her to
help Aspatria with such preparations as
could be made. But neither to her nor
yet to Aspatria did he speak of Fenwick's
avowed intention to leave his wife after the
ceremony. In the first place, he did not
believe that Fenwick would dare to give
him such a cowardly insult; and then,
also, he thought that the sight of Aspatria's suffering would make him tender
toward her. William Anneys's simple,
kindly soul did not understand that of all
things the painful results of our sins are
the most irritating. The hatred we ought
to give to the sin or to the sinner, we give
to the results.

Surely it was the saddest preparation
for a wedding that could be. Will and
Brune were " out." They did not speak to
each other, except about the farm business.
Aspatria spent most of her time in her
own room with a sempstress, who was
making the long-delayed wedding-dress.

The silk for it had been bought more than
a year, and it had lost some of its lustrous
colour. Mrs. Frostham paid a short visit
every day, and occasionally Alice Frostham came with her. She was a very
pretty girl, gentle and affectionate to Aspatria; and just because of her kindness
Will determined at some time to make her
Mistress of Seat-Ambar.

But in the house there was a great depression, a depression that no one could
avoid feeling. Will gave no orders for
wedding-festivities; a great dinner and
ball would have been a necessity under the
usual circumstances, but there were no
arrangements even for a breakfast. Aspatria wondered at the omission, but she did
not dare to question Will; indeed, Will
appeared to avoid her as much as he
could.

Really, William Anneys was very anxious and miserable. He had no depen-
dence upon Fenwick's promise, and he
felt that if Fenwick deceived him there
was nothing possible but the last ven-

7

geance. He had this thought constantly
in his mind; and he was
quietly ordering
things on the
farm for a long
absence, and
for Brune's
management
or succession.
He paid several
visits to White-
haven, where was
his banker, and to
Gosport, where his law-
yer lived.   He felt, during
that terrible interval of suspense, very much as a man
under sentence of death
might feel.

The morning of the
fifteenth broke chill and   dark,
with a promise of rain.   Great
Gable was carrying   on a con-
flict with an army   of gray clouds
assailing h i s   summit and bod-

ing no good for the weather. The fog
rolled and eddied from side to side of the
mountains, which projected their black
forms against a ghastly, neutral tint behind
them; and the air was full of that melancholy stillness which so often pervades the
last days of autumn.

Squire Anneys had slept little for two
weeks, and he had been awake all the
night before. While yet very early, he
had every one in the house called. Still
there were no preparations for company
or feasting. Brune came down grumbling
at a breakfast by candle-light, and he and
William drank their coffee and made a
show of eating almost in silence. But
there was an unspeakable tenderness in
William's heart, if he had known how to
express it. He looked at Brune with a
new speculation in his eyes. Brune might
soon be master of Ambar-Side: what
kind of a master would he make? Would
he be loving to Aspatria? When Brune
had sons to inherit the land, would he
remember his promise, and avenge the

insult to the Anneys, if he, William, should
give his life in vain? Out of these questions many others arose; but he was naturally a man of few words, and not able to
talk himself into a conviction that he
was doing right; nor yet was he able to
give utterance to the vague objections
which, if defined by words, might perhaps have changed his feelings and his
plans.

He had sent Aspatria word that she
must be ready by ten o'clock. At eight
she began to dress. Her sleep had been
broken and miserable. She looked anxiously in the glass at her face. It was as
white as the silk robe she was to wear. A
feeling of dislike of the unhappy garment
rose in her heart. She had bought the
silk in the very noon of her love and
hopes, a shining piece of that pearl-like
tint which only the most brilliant freshness
and youth can becomingly wear. Many
little accessories were wanting. She tried
the Roman cameos with it, and they
looked heavy; she knew in her womanly

heart that it needed the lustre of gems, the
sparkle of diamonds or rubies.

Mrs. Frostham came a little later, and
assisted her in her toilet; but a passing
thought of the four bridemaids she had
once chosen for this office made her eyes
dim, while the stillness of the house, the
utter neglect of all symbols of rejoicing,
gave an ominous and sorrowful atmosphere
to the bride-robing. Still, Aspatria looked
very handsome; for as the melancholy
toilet offices proceeded with so little interest and so little sympathy, a sense of
resentment had gradually gathered in the
poor girl's heart. It made her carry herself proudly, it brought a flush to her
cheeks, and a flashing, trembling light to
her eyes which Mrs. Frostham could not
comfortably meet.

A few minutes before ten, she threw over
all her fateful finery a large white cloak,
which added a decided grace and dignity
to her appearance. It was a garment
Ulfar had sent her from London, — a long,
mantle-like wrap, made of white cashmere,

and lined with quilted white satin. Long
cords and tassels of chenille fastened it at
the throat, and the hood was trimmed with
soft white fur. She drew the hood over
her head, she felt glad to hide the wreath
of orange-buds and roses which Mrs. Frostham had insisted upon her wearing, — the
sign and symbol of her maidenhood.

Will looked at her with stern lips, but
as he wrapped up her satin-sandalled feet
in the carriage, he said softly to her, " God
bless you, Aspatria!" His voice trembled, but not more than Aspatria's as she
answered, —

" Thank you, Will. You and Brune are
father and mother to me to-day. There
is no one else."

" Never mind, my little lass. We are
enough."

She was alone in the carriage. Will
and Brune rode on either side of her. The
Frosthams, the Dawsons, the Bellendens,
the Atkinsons, and the Lutons followed.
Will had invited every one to the church,
and curiosity brought those who were not

moved by sympathy or regard.
Fortunately the rain held off,
though the air was damp and
exceedingly depressing.

When they arrived
at Aspatria Church,
they found the yard full;
every gravestone was occupied by a little party of
gossips. At the
gate there was
a handsome
travelling-
chariot
w i t h
f o u r
horses.
It lifted
a great
weight of
apprehen-   sion from
William   Anneys, for it
told him   that Fenwick had
kept his word.   He helped Aspatria
to alight, and his heart ached for her. How

would she be able to walk between that crowd of gazing, curious men and women? He held her arm tight against his big heart, and Brune, carefully watching her, followed close behind.

But Aspatria's inner self had taken possession of the outer woman. She walked firmly and proudly, with an erect grace, without hesitation and without hurry, toward her fate. Something within her kept saying words of love and encouragement; she knew not what they were, only they strengthened her like wine. She passed the church door whispering the promise given her, — "It is I. Be not afraid." And then her eyes fell upon the ancient stone font, at which her father and mother had named her. She put out her hand and just touched its holy chalice.

The church was crowded with a curious and not unsympathetic congregation. · Aspatria Anneys was their own, a daleswoman by a thousand years of birthright. Fenwick was a stranger. If he were going to do her any wrong, and Will Anneys was ready to punish him for it, every man and woman present would have stood shoulder to shoulder with Will. There was an undefined expectation of something unusual, of something more than a wedding. This feeling, though unexpressed, made itself felt in a very pronounced way. Will and Brune looked confidingly around; Aspatria gathered courage with every step. She felt that she was among her own people, living and dead.

As soon as they really entered the church, they saw Fenwick. He was with an officer wearing the uniform of the Household Troops; and he was evidently pointing out to him the ancient tombs of the Ambar-Anneys family, the Crusaders in stone, with sheathed swords and hands folded in prayer, and those of the family abbots, adorned with richly floriated crosses.

When he saw Aspatria he bowed, and advanced rapidly to the altar. She had loosened her cloak and flung back her hood, and she watched his approach with eyes that seemed two separate souls of love and sorrow. One glance from them troubled him to the seat of life. He motioned to the waiting clergyman, and took his place beside his bride. There was a dead stillness in the church, and a dead stillness outside; the neighing of a horse sounded sharp, imperative, fateful. A ripple of a smile followed; it was a lucky omen to hear a horse neigh. Brune glanced at his sister, but she had not heeded it. Her whole being was swallowed up in the fact that she was standing at Ulfar's side, that she was going to be his wife.

The aged clergyman was fumbling with the Prayer Book: "The Form of Solemnization of Matrimony" seemed hard to find. And so vagrant is thought, that while he turned the leaves Aspatria remembered the travelling-chariot, and wondered whether Ulfar meant to carry her away in it, and what she would do for proper clothing. Will ought to have told her something of the future. How cruel every one had been! It took but a moment for these and many other thoughts to invade Aspatria's heart, and spread dismay and anxiety and again the sense of resentment.

Then she heard the clergyman begin. His voice was like that of some one speaking in a dream, till she sharply called herself together, hearing also Ulfar's voice, and knowing that she too would be called upon for her assent. She glanced up at Ulfar, who was dressed with great care and splendour and looking very handsome, and said her "I will" with the glance. Ulfar could not receive it unmoved; he looked steadily at her, and then he saw the ruin of youth that his faithlessness had made. Remorse bit him like a serpent, but remorse is not repentance. Then William Anneys gave his sister to his enemy; and the gift was like death to him, and the look accompanying the gift filled Ulfar's heart with a contemptuous anger fatal to all juster or kinder feelings.

When the service was ended, Fenwick turned to Aspatria and offered her his hand. She put hers into his, and so he led her down the aisle, and through the church-yard, to her own carriage. William had followed close. He wondered if Fenwick meant to take his wife with him, and he resolved to give him the opportunity to do so. But as soon as he perceived that the bridegroom would carry out his threat, and desert his bride at the church gates, he stepped forward and said, —

"That is enough, Sir Ulfar Fenwick. I have made you keep your word. I will care for your wife. She shall neither bear your name nor yet take anything from your bounty."

Fenwick paid no heed to his brother-in-law. He looked at Aspatria. She was whiter than snow; she had the pallor of death. He lifted his hat and said, —

"Farewell, Lady Fenwick. We shall meet no more."

"Sir Ulfar," she answered calmly, "it is not my will that we met here to-day."

"And as for meeting no more," said Brune, with passionate contempt, "I will warrant that is not in your say-so, Ulfar Fenwick."

As he spoke, Fenwick's friend handed Will Anneys a card; then they drove rapidly away. Will was carefully wrapping his sister for her solitary ride back to Scat-Ambar; and he did this with forced deliberation, trying to appear undisturbed by what had occurred; for, since it had happened, he wished his neighbours to think he had fully expected it. And while so engaged he found opportunity to whisper to Aspatria: "Now, my little lass, bear up as bravely as may be. It is only one hour. Only one hour, dearie! Don't you try to speak. Only keep your head high till you get home, darling!"

So the sad procession turned homeward, Aspatria sitting alone in her carriage, William and Brune riding on either side of her, the squires and dames bidden to the ceremony following slowly behind. Some talked softly of the affair; some passionately assailed William Anneys for not felling the villain where he stood. Gradu-

ally they said good-by, and so went to their
own homes. Aspatria had to speak to
each, she had to sit erect, she had to bear
the wondering, curious gaze not only of

her friends, but of the hinds and peasant-
women in the small hamlets between the
church and Seat-Ambar; she had to endure her own longing and disappointment,
and make a poor attempt to smile when
the children flung their little posies of late
flowers into the passing carriage.

To the last moment she bore it. "A

good, brave girl!" said Will, as he left her
at her own room door. "My word! it is
better to have good blood than good
fortune: good blood never was beat!
Aspatria is only a little lass, but she is
more than a match for yon villain! A big
villain he is, a villain with a latchet!"

The miserable are sacred. All through
that wretched afternoon no one troubled
Aspatria. Will and Brune sat by the
parlour fire, for the most part silent. The
rain, which had barely held off until their
return from the church, now beat against
the window-panes, and drenched and scattered even the hardy Michaelmas daisies.
The house was as still as if there had been
death instead of marriage in it. Now and
then Brune spoke, and sometimes William
answered him, and sometimes he did not.

At last, after a long pause, Brune asked:
"What was it Fenwick's friend gave you?
A message?"

"A message."

"You might as well say what, Will."

"Ay, I might. It said Fenwick would

wait for me a week at the Sceptre Inn, Carlisle."

"Will you go to Carlisle?"

"To be sure I will go. I would not miss the chance of 'throwing' him, — no, 'not for ten years' life!"

"Dear me! what a lot of trouble has come with just taking a stranger in out of the storm!"

"Ay, it is a venturesome thing to do. How can any one tell what a stranger may bring in with him?"

CHAPTER IV.

FOR MOTHER'S SAKE.

IN the upper chamber where Will had left his sister, a great mystery of sorrow was being endured. Aspatria felt as if all had been. Life had no more joy to give, and no greater grief to inflict. She undressed with rapid, trembling fingers; her wedding finery was hateful in her sight. On the night before she had folded all her store of clothing, and laid it ready to put in a trunk. She had been quite in the dark as to her destiny; the only thing that appeared certain to her was that she would have to leave home. Perhaps she would go with Ulfar from the church door. In that case Will would have to send her clothing, and she had laid it in the neatest order for the emergency.

On the top of one pile lay a crimson Canton crape shawl. Her mother had worn it constantly during the last year of her life; and Aspatria had put it away, as something too sacred for ordinary use. She now folded it around her shoulders, and sat down. Usually, when things troubled her, she was restless and kept in motion, but this trouble was too bitter and too great to resist; she was quiet, she took its blows passively, and they smote her on every side.

Could she ever forget that cruel ride home, ever cease to burn and shiver when she remembered the eyes that had scanned her during its progress? The air seemed full of them. She covered her face to avoid the pitying, wondering, scornful glances. But this ride through the valley of humiliation was not the bitterest drop in her bitter cup; she could have smiled as she rode and drank it, if Ulfar had been at her side. It was his desertion that was so distracting to her. She had thought of many sorrows in connection with this forced marriage, but this sorrow had never suggested itself as possible.

Therefore, when Ulfar bade her farewell she had felt as if standing on the void of the universe. It was the superhuman woman within her that had answered him, and that had held up her head and had strengthened her for her part all through that merciless ride. And the sight of her handsome, faithless lover, the tones of his voice, the touch of his hand, his half-respectful, half-pitying kindness, had awakened in her heart a tenfold love for him.

For she understood then, for the first time, her social and educational inferiority. She felt even that she had done herself less than justice in her fine raiment: her country breeding and simple beauty would have appeared to greater advantage in the white merino she had desired to wear. She had been forced into a dress that accentuated her deficiencies. At that hour she thought she could never see Mrs. Frostham again.

To these tempestuous, humiliating, heart-breaking reflections the storm outside made an angry accompaniment. The

wind howled down the chimney and wailed
around the house, and the rain beat
against the window and pattered on the
flagged walks.
The darkness
came on early,
and the cold grew
every hour more
searching.   She
was not insen-
sible to these
physical dis-
comforts, but
they seemed
so small a
part of her
misery that
she made no
resistance to
their attack.
Will and Brune,
sitting   almost speechless
downstairs, were both thinking of her.
When it was quite dark they grew unhappy.   First one and then the other

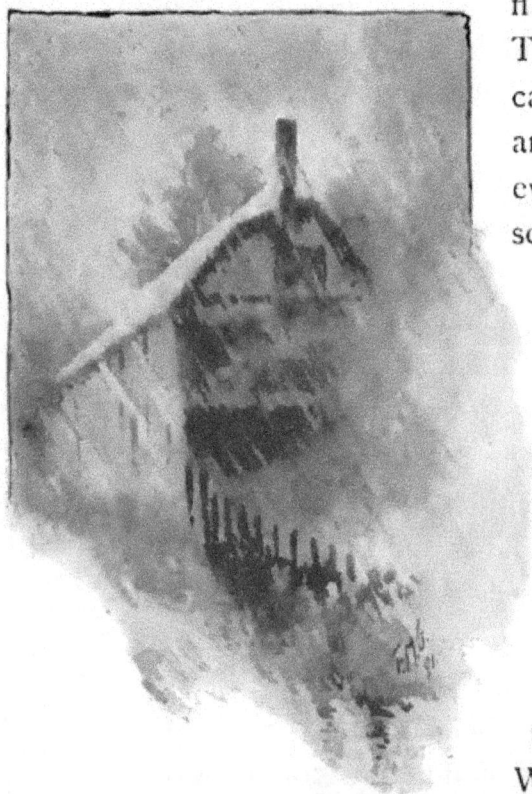

crept softly to her room door. All was as still as death. No movement, no sound of any kind, betrayed in what way the poor soul within suffered. No thread of light came from beneath the door: she was in the dark, and she had eaten nothing all day.

About six o'clock Will could bear it no longer. He knocked softly at her door, and said: "My little lass, speak to Will! Have a cup of tea! Do have a cup of tea, dearie!"

The voice was so unlike Will's voice that it startled Aspatria. It told her of a suffering almost equalling her own. She rose from the chair in which she had been sitting for hours, and went to him. The room was dark, the passage was dark; he saw nothing but the denser dark of her figure, and her white face above it. She saw nothing but his great bulk and his shining eyes. But she felt the love flowing out from his heart to her, she felt his sorrow and his sympathy, and it comforted her. She said: "Will, do not fret about me. I am over-getting the shame and sorrow. Yes, I will have a cup of tea, and tell Tabitha to make a fire here. Dear Will, I have been a great care and shame to you."

"Ay, you have, Aspatria; but I would rather die than miss you, my little lass."

This interview gave a new bent to Aspatria's thoughts. As she drank the tea, and warmed her chilled feet before the blaze, she took into consideration what misery her love for Ulfar Fenwick had brought to her brothers' once happy home, the anxiety, the annoyance, the shame, the ill-will and quarrelling, the humiliations that Will and Brune had been compelled to endure. Then suddenly there flashed across her mind the card given to Will by Ulfar's friend. She was not too simple to conceive of its meaning. It was a defiance of some kind, and she knew how Will would answer it. Her heart stood still with terror.

She had seen Will and Ulfar wrestling; she had heard Will say to Brune, when Ulfar was absent, "He knows little about it; when I had that last grip, I could have flung him into eternity." It was common enough for dalesmen quarrelling to have a "fling" with one another and stand by its results. If Will and Ulfar met thus, one or both would be irremediably injured. In their relation to her, both were equally dear. She would have given her poor little life cheerfully for the love of either. Her cup shook in her hand. She had a sense of hurry in the matter, that drove her like a leaf before a strong wind. If Will got to bed before she saw him, he might be away in the morning ere she was aware. She put down her cup, and while she stood a moment to collect her strength and thoughts, the subject on all its sides flashed clearly before her.

A minute afterward she opened the parlour door. Brune sat bent forward, with a poker in his hands. He was tracing a woman's name in the ashes, though he was hardly conscious of the act. Will's head was thrown back against his chair; he seemed to be asleep. But when Aspatria opened the door, he sat upright and looked at her. A pallor like death spread over his face; it was the crimson shawl, his mother's shawl, which caused it. Wearing it, Aspatria closely resembled her. Will had idolized his mother in life, and he worshipped her memory. If Aspatria had considered every earthly way of touching Will's heart, she could have selected none so certain as the shawl, almost accidentally assumed.

She went direct to Will. He drew a low stool to his side, and Aspatria sat down upon it, and then stretched out her left hand to Brune. The two men looked at their sister, and then they looked at each other. The look was a vow. Both so understood it.

"Will and Brune," the girl spoke softly, but with a great steadiness, — "Will and Brune, I am sorry to have given you so much shame and trouble."

"It is not your fault, Aspatria," said Brune.

"But I will do so no more. I will never

name Ulfar again. I will try to be cheerful and to make home cheerful, try to carry on life as it used to be before he came. We will not let people talk of him, we will not mind it if they do. Eh, Will?"

"Just now, dear, in a little while."

"Will, dear Will! what did that card mean, — the one Ulfar's friend gave? You will not go near Ulfar, Will? Please do not!"

"I have a bit of business to settle with him, Aspatria, and then I never want to see his face again."

"Will, you must not go."

"Ay, but I must. I have been thought of with a lot of bad names, but no one shall think 'coward' of me."

"Will, remember all I have suffered to-day."

"I am not likely to forget it."

"That ride home, Will, was as if I was going up Calvary. My wedding-dress was heavy as a cross, and that foolish wreath of flowers was a wreath of cruel thorns. I was pitied and scorned, till I

felt as if my heart — my real heart — was
all bruised and torn. I have suffered
so much, Will, spare me more suffering.
Will! Will! for your little sister's sake,
put that card in the fire, and stay here,
right here with me."

"My lass! my dear lass, you cannot tell
what you are asking."

"I am asking you to give up your revenge. I know that is a great thing for
a man to do. But, Will, dear, you stand
in father's place, you are sitting in father's
chair; what would he say to you?"

"He would say, 'Give the rascal a good
thrashing, Will. When a man wrongs a
woman, there is no other punishment for
him. Thrash him to within an inch of his
cruel, selfish, contemptible life!' That is
what father would say, Aspatria. I know
it, I feel it."

"If you will not give up your revenge
for me, nor yet for father, then I ask you
for mother's sake! What would mother
say to-night if she were here? — very like
she is here. Listen to her, Will. She is

saying, ' Spare my little girl any more sorrow and shame, Will, my boy Will!'— that is what mother would say. And if you hurt Ulfar you hurt me also, and if Ulfar hurts you my heart will break. The. fell-side is ringing now with my troubles. If I have any more, I will go away where no one can find me. For mother's sake, Will! For mother's sake!"

The strong man was sobbing behind his hands, the struggle was a terrific one. Brune watched it with tears streaming unconsciously down his cheeks. Aspatria sunk at Will's feet, and buried her face on his knees.

" For mother's sake, Will! Let Ulfar go free."

" My dear little lass, I cannot!"

" For mother's sake, Will! I am speaking for mother! For mother's sake!"

" I — I — Oh, what shall I do, Brune?"

" For mother's sake, Will!"

He trembled until the chair shook. He dared not look at the weeping girl. She rose up. She gently moved away his hands. She kissed his eyelids. She said, with an irresistible entreaty: " Look at me, Will. I am speaking for mother. Let Ulfar alone. I do not say forgive him."

" Nay, I will never forgive him."

" But let him alone. Will! Will! let him alone, for mother's sake !"

Then he stood up. He looked into Aspatria's eyes; he let his gaze wander to the crimson shawl. He began to sob like a child.

"You may go, Aspatria," he said, in broken words. " If you ask me anything in mother's name, I have no power to say no."

He walked to the window and looked out into the dark stormy night, and Brune motioned to Aspatria to go away. He knew Will would regain himself better in her absence. She was glad to go. As soon as Will had granted her request, she fell to the lowest ebb of life. She could hardly drag herself up the long, dark stairs. She dropped asleep as soon as she reached her room.

It was a bitter awakening. The soul feels sorrow keenest at the first moments of con- sciousness. It has been away, perhaps, in happy scenes, or it has been lulling itself in deep repose, and then suddenly it is called to lift again the heavy burden of its daily life. Aspa- tria stood in her cold, dim room; and even while shivering in her thin night-dress, with bare feet treading the polished oak floor, she hastily put out of her sight the miserable wedding-garments. A large dower-chest stood conveniently near. She opened it wide, and flung dress and wreath and slippers and cloak into it. The lid fell from her hands with a great clang, and

she said to herself, "I will never open it again."

The storm still continued. She dressed in simple household fashion, and went downstairs. Brune sat by the fire. He said: "I was waiting for you, Aspatria. Will is in the barn. He had his coffee and bacon long ago."

"Brune, will you be my friend through all this trouble?"

"I will stand by you through thick and thin, Aspatria. There is my hand on it."

About great griefs we do not chatter; and there was no further discussion of those events which had been barely turned away from tragedy and death. Murder and despairing love and sorrow might have a secret dwelling-place in Seat-Ambar, but it was in the background. The front of life went on as smoothly as ever; the cows were milked, the sheep tended, the men and maids had their tasks, the beds were made, and the tables set, with the usual order and regularity.

And Aspatria found this "habit of living" to be a good staff to lean upon. She assumed certain duties, and performed them; and the house was pleasanter for her oversight. Will and Brune came far oftener to sit at the parlour fireside, when they found Aspatria there to welcome them. And so the days and weeks followed one another, bringing with them those commonplace duties and interests which give to existence a sense of stability and order. No one spoke of Fenwick; but all the more Aspatria nursed his image in her heart and her imagination. He had dressed himself for his marriage with great care and splendour. Never had he looked so handsome and so noble in her eyes, and never until that hour had she realized her social inferiority to him, her lack of polish and breeding, her ignorance of all things which a woman of birth and wealth ought to know and to possess.

This was a humiliating acknowledgment; but it was Aspatria's first upward step, for with it came an invincible deter-

mination to make herself worthy of her
husband's love and companionship. The
hope and the object gave a new colour to
her life. As she went about her simple
duties, as she sat alone in her room, as
she listened to her brothers talking, it
occupied, strengthened, and inspired her.
Dark as the present was, it held the hope
of a future which made her blush and
tingle to its far-off joy. To learn everything, to go everywhere, to become a
brilliant woman, a woman of the world, to
make her husband admire and adore her, —
these were the dreams that brightened the
long, sombre winter, and turned the low
dim rooms into a palace of enchantment.

She was aware of the difficulties in her
way. She thought first of asking Will to
permit her to go to a school in London.
But she knew he would never consent.
She had no friends to whom she could
confide her innocent plans, she had as yet
no money in her own control. But in less
than two years she would be of age. Her
fortune would then be at her disposal, and

the law would permit her to order her own
life. In the mean time she could read and
study at home: when the spring came
she would see the vicar, and he would
lend her books from his library.
There was an Encyclopædia in
the house; she got to-
gether its scattered
volumes, and began
to make herself
familiar with its
mélange of in-
formation.

In such efforts
her heart was
purified from
all bitterness,
wounded vanity,
and impatience. Life
was neither lonely nor
monotonous, she had a noble
object to work for. So the winter
passed, and the spring came again. All
over the fells the ewes and their lambs
made constant work for the shepherds;

and Aspatria greatly pleased Will by going out frequently to pick up the perishing, weakly lambs and succour them.

One day in April she took a bottle of warm milk and a bit of sponge and went up Calder Fell. On the first reach of the fell she found a dying lamb, and carried it down to the shelter of some whin-bushes. Then she fed it with the warm milk, and the little creature went to sleep in her arms.

The grass was green and fresh, the sun warm; the whins sheltered her from the wind, and a little thrush in them, busy building her nest, was making sweet music out of air as sweet. All was so glad and quiet: she, too, was happy in her own thoughts. A wagon passed, and then a tax-cart, and afterward two old men going ditching. She hardly lifted her head; every one knew Aspatria Anneys. When the shadows told her that it was near noon, she rose to go home, holding the lamb in her arms. At that moment a carriage came slowly from behind the hedge. She

saw the fine horses with their glittering
harness, and knew it was a strange vehicle

in Ambar-Side, so she sat down
again until it should pass. The lamb was
in her left arm. She threw back her head,

and gazed fixedly into the whin-bush where the thrush had its nest. Whoever it was, she did not wish to be recognized.

Lady Redware, Sarah Sandys, and Ulfar Fenwick were in the carriage. At the moment she stood with the lamb in her arms, Ulfar had known his wife. Lady Redware saw her almost as quickly, and in some occult way she transferred, by a glance, the knowledge to Sarah. The carriage was going very slowly; the beauty of the thrown-back head, the simplicity of her dress, the pastoral charm of her position, all were distinct. Ulfar looked at her with a fire of passion in his eyes, Lady Redware with annoyance. Sarah asked, with a mocking laugh, "Is that really Little Bo Peep?" The joke fell flat. Ulfar did not immediately answer it; and Sarah was piqued.

"I shall go to Italy again," she said. "Englishmen may be admirable *en masse*, but individually they are stupid or cross."

"In Italy there are the Capuchins," answered Ulfar. He remembered that Sarah had expressed herself strongly about the order.

"I have just passed a week at Oxford among the Reverends; all things considered, I prefer the Capuchins. When you have dined with a lord bishop, you want to become a socialist."

"Your Oxford friends are very nice people, Sarah."

"Excellent people, Elizabeth, quite superior people, and they are all sure not only of going to heaven, but also of joining the very best society the place affords."

"Best society!" said Ulfar, pettishly. "I am going to America. There, I hope, I shall hear nothing about it."

"America is so truly admirable. Why was it put in such an out-of-the-way place? You have to sail three thousand miles to get to it," pouted Sarah.

"All things worth having are put out of the way," replied Ulfar.

"Yes," sighed Sarah. "What an admirable story is that of the serpent and the apple!"

"Come, Ulfar!" said Lady Redware, "do try to be agreeable. You used to be so delightful! Was he not, Sarah?"

"Was he? I have forgotten, Elizabeth. Since that time a great deal of water has run into the sea."

"If you want an ill-natured opinion about yourself, by all means go to a woman for it." And Ulfar enunciated this dictum with a very scornful shrug of his shoulders.

"Ulfar!"

"It is so, Elizabeth."

"Never mind him, dear!" said Sarah. "I do not. And I have noticed that the men who give bad characters to women have usually much worse ones themselves. I think Ulfar is quite ready for American society and its liberal ideas." And Sarah drew her shawl into her throat, and looked defiantly at Ulfar.

"The Americans are all socialists. I have read that, Ulfar. You know what these liberal ideas come to, — always socialism."

"Do not be foolish, Elizabeth. Socialism never comes from liberality of thought: it is always a bequest of tyranny."

"Ulfar, when are you going to be really nice and good again?"

"I do not know, Elizabeth."

"Ulfar is a standing exception to the rule that when things are at their worst they must mend. Ulfar, lately, is always at his worst, and he never mends."

There was really some excuse for Ulfar; he was suffering keenly, and neither of the two women cared to recognize the fact. He had just returned from Italy with his father's remains, and after their burial he had permitted Elizabeth to carry him off with her to Redware. In reality the neighbourhood of Aspatria drew him like a magnet. He had been haunted by her last, resentful, amazed, miserable look. He understood from it that Will had never told her of his intention to bid her farewell as soon as she was his wife, and he was not devoid of imagination. His mind had constantly pictured scenes of humiliation which he had condemned the woman he had once so tenderly loved to endure.

And that passing glimpse of her under the whin-bushes had revived something of his old passion. He answered his sister's and Sarah's remarks pettishly, because he wanted to be left alone with the new hope that had come to him. Why not take Aspatria to America? She was his wife. He had been compelled, by his sense of justice and honour, to make her Lady Fenwick; why should he deny himself her company, merely to keep a passionate, impulsive threat?

To the heart the past is eternal, and love survives the pang of separation. He thought of Aspatria for the next twenty-four hours. To see her! to speak to her! to hear her voice! to clasp her to his heart! Why should he deny himself these delights? What pleasure could pride and temper give him in exchange? Fenwick had always loved to overcome an obstacle, and such people cannot do without obstacles; they are a necessary aliment.

To see and to speak with Aspatria was now the one thing in life worthy of his attention.

It was not an easy thing to accomplish. Every day for nearly a week he rode furiously to Calder Wood, tied his horse there, and then hung about the brow of Calder Cliff, for it commanded Seat-Ambar, which lay below it as the street lies below a high tower. With his glass he could see and Brune passing house to the barns and once he saw meet her brother lift her face to Will put her and so go How he What a Will from the or the fields, Aspatria go to Will; he saw her Will's face, he saw arm through his arm with her to the house. hated Will Anneys! triumph it would be to carry off his sister unknown to him and without his say-so!

One morning he determined if he found no opportunity to see Aspatria that day alone he would risk all, and go boldly to the house. Why should he not do so? He had scarcely made the decision when he saw Will and Brune drive away together. He remembered it was Dalton market-day; and he knew that they had gone there. Almost immediately Aspatria left the house also. Then he was jealous. Where was she going as soon as her brothers left her? She was going to the vicar's to return a book and carry him a cream cheese of her own making.

He knew then how to meet her. She would pass through a meadow on her way home, and this meadow was skirted by a young plantation. Half-way down there was a broad stile between the two. He hurried his steps, and arrived there just as Aspatria entered the meadow. There was a high frolicking wind blowing right in her face. It had blown her braids loose, and her tippet and dress backward; her slim form was sharply defined by it, and it compelled her to hold up both her hands in order to keep her hat on her head.

She came on so, treading lightly, almost dancing with the merry gusts to and fro. Once Ulfar heard a little cry that was half laughter, as the wind made her pirouette and then stand still to catch her breath. Ulfar thought the picture bewitching. He waited until she was within a yard or two of the stile, ere he crossed it. She was holding her hat down: she did not see him until he could have put his hand upon her. Then she let her hands fall, and her hat blew backward, and she stood quite still and quite speechless, her colour coming and going, all a woman's softest witchery beaming in her eyes.

"Aspatria! dear Aspatria! I am come to take you with me. I am going to America." He spoke a little sadly, as if he had some reason for feeling grieved.

She shook her head positively, but she did not, or she could not, speak.

" Aspatria, have you no kiss, no word of

welcome, no love to give me?" And he put out his hand, as if to draw her to his embrace.

She stepped quickly backward: "No, no, no! Do not touch me, Ulfar. Go away. Please go away!"

"But you must go with me. You are my wife, Aspatria." And he said the last words very like a command.

"I am not your wife. Oh, no!"

"I say you are. I married you in Aspatria Church."

"You also left me there, left me to such shame and sorrow as no man gives to the woman he loves."

"Perhaps I did act cruelly in two or three ways, Aspatria; but people who love forgive two or three offences. Let us be lovers as we used to be."

"No, I will not be lovers as we used to be. People who love do not commit two or three such offences as you committed against me."

"I will atone for them. I will indeed! Aspatria, I miss you very much. I will

not go to America without you. How
soon can you be ready? In a week?"

"You will atone to me? How? There
is but one way. You shall, in your own
name, call every one in Allerdale, gentle
and simple, to Aspatria Church. You
shall marry me again in their presence,
and go with me to my own home. The
wedding-feast shall be held there. You
shall count Will and Brune Anneys as
your brothers. You shall take me away,
in the sight of all, to your home. Of all
the honour a wife ought to have you must
give me here, among my own people, a
double portion. Will you do this in
atonement?"

"You are talking folly, Aspatria. I
have married you once."

"You have not married me once. You
met me at Aspatria Church to shame me,
to break my heart with love and sorrow,
to humble my good brothers. No, I am
not your wife! I will not go with you!"

"I can make you go, Aspatria. You
seem to forget the law —"

"Will says the law will protect me. But if it did not, if you took me by force to your house or yacht, you would not have me. You could not touch me. Aspatria Anneys is beyond your reach."

"You are Aspatria Fenwick."

"I have never taken your name. Will told me not to do so. Anneys is a good name. No Anneys ever wronged me."

"You refused my home, you refused my money, and now you refuse my name. You are treating me as badly as possible. The day before our marriage I sent to your brother a signed settlement for your support, the use of Fenwick Castle as a residence, and two thousand pounds a year. Your brother Will, the day after our marriage, took it to my agent and tore it to pieces in his presence."

"Will did right. He knew his sister would not have your home and money without your love."

She spoke calmly, with a dignity that became well her youth and beauty. Ulfar thought her exceedingly lovely. He attempted to woo her again with the tender glances and soft tones and caressing touch of their early acquaintance. Aspatria sorrowfully withdrew herself; she held only repelling palms toward his bending face. She was not coy, he could have overcome coyness; she was cold, and calm, and watchful of him and of herself. Her face and throat paled and blushed, and blushed and paled; her eyes were dilated with feeling; her pretty bow-shaped mouth trembled; she radiated a personality sweet, strong, womanly, — a piquant, woodland, pastoral delicacy, all her own.

But after many useless efforts to influence her, he began to despair. He perceived that she still loved him, perhaps better than she had ever done, but that her determination to consider their marriage void had its source in a oneness of mind having no second thoughts and no doubt behind it. The only hope she gave him was in another marriage ceremony which in its splendour and publicity should atone in some measure for the first. He

could not contemplate such a confession
of his own fault. He could not give Will
and Brune Anneys such a triumph. If
Aspatria loved him, how could she ask
such a humiliating atonement? Aspatria
saw the shadow of these reflections on his
face. Though he said nothing, she understood it was this struggle that gave the
momentary indecision to his pleading.

For herself, she did not desire a present
reconciliation. She had nursed too long
the idea of the Aspatria that was to be, the
wise, clever, brilliant woman who was to
win over again her husband. She did not
like to relinquish this hope for a present
gratification, a gratification so much lower
in its aim that she now understood that it
never could long satisfy a nature so complex and so changeable as Ulfar's. She
therefore refused him his present hope,
believing that fate had a far better meeting
in store for them.

While these thoughts flashed through
her mind, she kept her eyes upon the
horizon. In that wide-open fixed gaze her

loving, troubled soul revealed itself. Ulfar was wondering whether it was worth while to begin his argument all over again, when she said softly: "We must now say farewell. I see the vicar's maid coming. In a few hours the fell-side will know of our meeting. I must tell Will, myself. I entreat you to leave the dales as soon as possible."

"I will not leave them without you."

"Go to-night. I shall not change what I have said. There is nothing to be done but to part. We are no longer alone. Good-by, Ulfar!—dear Ulfar!"

"I care not who is present. You are my wife." And he clasped her in his arms and kissed her.

Perhaps she was not sorry. Perhaps her own glance of love and longing had commanded the embrace; for when she released herself she was weeping, and Ulfar's tears were on her cheeks. But she called the vicar's maid imperatively, and so put an end to the interview.

"That was my husband, Lottie," she

said. It was the only explanation offered. Aspatria knew it was useless to expect any reticence on the subject. In that isolated valley such a piece of news could not be kept; the very birds would talk about it in their nests. She must herself tell Will, and although she had done nothing wrong, she was afraid to tell him.

When she reached home she was glad to hear that Will had been sent for to Squire Frostham's. "It was something about a fox," said Brune. "They wanted me too, but Alice Frostham is a girl I cannot abide. I would not go near her."

"Brune, will you take a long ride for my sake?"

"I will do anything for you I can."

"I met Ulfar Fenwick this morning."

"Then you did a bad thing. I would not have believed it of you. Good Lord! there is as much two-facedness in a woman as there is meat in an egg."

"Brune, you are thinking wrong. I did not know he was in the country till he stood before me; and he did not move

me a hair's-breadth any way. But Lottie
from the vicarage saw us together; and
she was going to Dalton. You know what
she will say; and by and by the Frosthams
will hear; and then they will feel it to be
'only kind' to talk to Will about me and
my affairs; and the end of it will be some
foolish deed or other. If you love me,
Brune, go to Redware to-night, and see
Lady Redware, and tell her there is danger for her brother if he stays around
here."

"I can say that truly. There is danger
for the scoundrel, a good deal of it."

"Brune, it would be such a sorrow to
me if every one were talking of me again.
Do what I ask you, Brune. You promised
to stand by me through thick and thin."

"I did; and I will go to Redware as
soon as I have eaten my dinner. If Lottie
saw him, it will be known all over. And
if no one came up here on purpose to tell
Will, he would hear it at Dalton next week,
when that lot of bothering old squires sit
down to their market dinner. It would

be a grand bit for them to chew with their
victuals."

"I thought they talked about politics."

"They are like other men. If you get

more than one man in a
place, they are talking bad
about some woman. They
call it politics, but it is mostly
slander."

"I am going to tell Will myself."

"That is a deal the best plan."

"Be sure to frighten Lady Redware;
make her think Ulfar's life is in danger, —
anything to get him out of the dales."

"She will feel as if the heavens were
going to fall, when I get done with her.
My word! who would have thought of him
coming back? Life is full of surprises."

" But only think, if there was never anything accidental happened! Surprises are
just what make life worth having, — eh,
Brune?"

" Maybe so, and maybe not. When
Will comes home, tell him everything at
once. I can manage Lady Redware, I 'll
be bound."

With the promise he went away to per-
form it, and Aspatria carried her trembling
heart into solitude. But the lonely place
was full of Ulfar. A thousand hopes were
budding in her heart, growing slowly,
strongly, sweetly, in that earth which
she had made for them out of her love,
her desires, her hopes, and her faithful
aspirations.

CHAPTER V.

BUT THEY WERE YOUNG.

BRUNE arrived at Redware Hall while it was still afternoon, and he found no difficulty in obtaining an interview with its mistress. She was sitting at a table in a large bay-window, painting the view from it. For in those days ladies were not familiar with high art and all its nomenclature and accessories; Lady Redware had never thought of an easel, or a blouse, or indeed of any of the trappings now considered necessary to the making of pictures. She was prettily dressed in silk; and a square of bristol-board, a box of Newman's water-colours, and a few camel's-hair pencils were neatly arranged before her.

She rose when Brune entered, and met him with a suave courtesy; and the unso-

phisticated young man took it for a gen-
uine pleasure. He felt sorry to trouble
such a nice-looking gentlewoman, and he
said so with a sincerity that made her suddenly serious. "Have you brought me
bad news, Mr. Anneys?" she asked.

"I am afraid you will be put about a
bit. Sir Ulfar Fenwick met my sister this
morning; and they were seen by ill-natured
eyes, and I came, quiet-like, to let you know
that he must leave the dales to-night."

"Cannot Sir Ulfar meet his own wife?"

"Lady Redware, that is not the question. Put it, 'Cannot Sir Ulfar meet your
sister?' and I will answer you quick
enough, 'Not while there are two honest
men in Allerdale to prevent him.'"

"You cannot frighten Sir Ulfar from
Allerdale. To threaten him is to make
him stay."

"Dalesmen are not ones to threaten. I
tell you that the vicar's maid saw Sir Ulfar
and my sister together; and when William
Anneys hears of it, Sir Ulfar will get such
a notice to leave these parts as will give

him no choice. I came to warn him away before he could not help himself. I say freely, I did so to please Aspatria, and out of no good-will going his way."

"But if he will not leave Allerdale?"

"But if William Anneys, and the sixty gentlemen who will ride with William Anneys, say he must go? What then?"

"Of course Sir Ulfar cannot fight a mob."

"Not one of that mob of gentlemen would fight him; but they all carry stout riding-whips." And Brune looked at the lady with a sombre intentness which made further speech unnecessary. She had been alarmed from the first; she now made no further attempt to disguise her terror.

"What must I do, Mr. Anneys?" she asked. "What must I do?"

"Send your brother away from Cumberland to-night. I say he must leave to-night. To-morrow morning may be too late to prevent a great humiliation. Aspatria begged me to come to you. I do not say I wanted to come."

At this moment the door opened, and
Sarah Sandys entered. Brune turned, and
saw her; and his heart stood still. She
came slowly forward, her garment of pale-green and
white just touching
her sandalled feet.
She had a rush bas-
ket full of violets in
h e r hands; there
were primroses in
her breast and belt,
and her face was
like a pink rose.
High on her head her
fair hair was lifted, and,
being fastened w i t h a
large turquoise comb, it
gave the idea of sunshine and
blue sky.

Brune stood looking at her, as a mortal
might look at the divine Cytherea made
manifest. His handsome, open face, full
of candid admiration, had almost an august
character. He bowed to her, as men bow

when they bend their heart and give its
homage and delight. Sarah was much
impressed by the young man's beauty, and
she felt his swift adoration of her own
charms. She made Lady Redware intro-
duce her to Brune, and she completed her
conquest of the youth as she stood a
moment holding his hand and smiling with
captivating grace into his eyes.

Then Lady Redware explained Brune's
mission, and Sarah grasped the situation
without any disguises. "It simply means
flight, Elizabeth," she said. "What could
Ulfar do with fifty or sixty angry Cumberland squires? He would have to go. In
fact, I know they have a method of per-
suasion no mortal man can resist."

Brune saw that his errand was accom-
plished. Lady Redware thanked him for
his consideration, and Sarah rang for the
tea-service, and made him a cup, and gave
it to him with her own lovely hands.
Brune saw their exquisite form, their trans-
lucent glow, the sparkling of diamonds
and emeralds upon them. The tea was

as if brewed in Paradise; it tasted of all
things delightful; it was a veritable cup
of enchantments.

Then Brune rode away, and the two
women watched him over the hill. He
sat his great black hunter like a cavalry
officer; and the creature devoured the
distance with strides that made their hearts
leap to the sense of its power and life.

"He is the very handsomest man I ever
saw!" said Sarah.

"What is to be done about Ulfar?
Sarah, you must manage this business.
He will not listen to me."

"Ulfar has five senses. Ulfar is very
fond of himself. He will leave Redware,
of course. How handsome Brune Anneys
is!"

"Will you coax him to leave to-night?"

"Ulfar? Yes, I will; for it is the proper
thing for him to do. It would be a shame
to bring his quarrels to your house. — What
a splendid rider! Look, Elizabeth, he is
just topping the hill! I do believe he
turned his head! Is he not handsome?

Apollo! Antinoüs! Pshaw! Brune Anneys is a great deal more human, and a
great deal more godlike, than either."

"Do not be silly, Sarah. And do oc-
cupy yourself a little with Ulfar now."

"When the hour comes, I will. Ulfar
is evidently occupying himself at present
in watching his wife. There is a decorous
naughtiness and a stimulating sense of
danger about seeing Aspatria, that must
be a thorough enjoyment to Ulfar."

"Men are always in fusses. Ulfar has
kept my heart palpitating ever since he
could walk alone."

Sarah sighed. "It is very difficult,"
she said, "to decide whether very old men
or very young men can be the greater
trial. The suffering both can cause is immense! Poor Sandys was sixty-six, and
Ulfar is thirty-six, and — " She shook
her head, and sighed again.

"How hateful country-people are!" exclaimed Elizabeth. "They must talk, no
matter what tragedy they cause with their
scandalous words."

"Are they worse than our own set, either in town or country? You know what the Countess of Denbigh considered pleasant conversation? — telling things that ought not to be told."

"The Countess is a wretch! she would tell the most sacred of secrets."

"I tell secrets also. I do not consider it wrong. What business has any one to throw the *onus* of keeping their secret on my shoulders? Why should they expect from me more prudence than they themselves have shown?"

"That is true. But in these valleys they speak so uncomfortably direct; nothing but the strongest, straightest, most definite words will be used."

"That is a pity. People ought to send scandal through society in a respectable hunt-the-slipper form of circulation. But that is a kind of decency to be cultivated. However, I shall tell Ulfar, in the plainest words I can find, that there will be about sixty Cumberland squires here to-morrow, to ride with him out of the county, and

that they are looking forward to the fun
of it just as much as if it was a fox-hunt.
Ulfar has imagination. He will be able
to conceive such a ride, — the flying man,
and the roaring, laughing, whip-cracking
squires after him! He will remember
how Tom Appleton the wrestler, who did
something foul, was escorted across the
county line last summer. And Ulfar hates
a scene. Can you fancy him making himself the centre of such an affair? "

So they talked while Brune galloped
homeward in a very happy mood. He
felt as those ancients may have felt when
they met the Immortals and saluted them.
The thought of the beautiful Mrs. Sandys
filled his imagination; but he talked comfortably to Aspatria, and assured her that
there was now no fear of a meeting between her husband and Will. " Only," he
said, "tell Will yourself to-night, and he
will never doubt you."

Unfortunately, Will did not return that
night from the Frosthams'; for in the morning the two men were to go together to Dal-

ton very early. Will heard nothing there,
but Mrs. Frostham was waiting at her garden gate to tell him when he returned. He
had left Squire Frostham with his son-in-
law, and was alone. Mrs. Frostham made
a great deal of the information, and broke
it to Will with much consideration. Will
heard her sullenly. He was getting a few
words ready for Aspatria, as Mrs. Frostham told her tale, but they were for her
alone. To Mrs. Frostham he adopted a
tone she thought very ungrateful.

For when the whole affair, real and con-
sequential, had been told, he answered:
"What is there to make a wonder of?
Cannot a woman talk and walk a bit with
her own husband? Maybe he had something very particular to say to her. I think
it is a shame to bother a little lass about a
thing like that."

And he folded himself so close that Mrs.
Frostham could neither question nor sympathize with him longer. "Good-evening
to you," he said coldly; and then, while
visible, he took care to ride as if quite at

his ease. But the moment the road turned
from Frostham he whipped his horse to
its full speed, and entered the farmyard
with it in a foam of hurry, and himself
in a foam of passion.

Aspatria met him with the confession on
her lips. He gave her no time. He assailed her with affronting and injurious
epithets. He pushed her hands and face
from him. He vowed her tears were a
mockery, and her intention of confessing a
lie. He met all her efforts at explanation,
and all her attempts to pacify him, at
sword-point.

She bore it patiently for a while; and
then Will Anneys saw an Aspatria he had
never dreamed of. She seemed to grow
taller; she did really grow taller; her face
flamed, her eyes flashed, and, in a voice
authoritative and irresistible, she commanded him to desist.

"You are my worst enemy," she said.
"You are as deaf as the village gossips.
You will not listen to the truth. Your
abuse, heard by every servant in the house,

certifies all that malice dares to think.
And in wounding my honour you are
a parricide to our mother's good name!
I am ashamed of you, Will!"

From head to foot she reflected the in-
dignation in her heart, as she stood erect
with her hands clasped and the palms
dropped downward, no sign of tears, no
quiver of fear or doubt, no retreat, and no
submission, in her face or attitude.

"Why, whatever is the matter with you,
Aspatria?"

At this moment Brune entered, and she
went to him, and put her hand through
his arm, and said: "Brune, speak for me!
Will has insulted mother and father,
through me, in such a way that I can
never forgive him!"

"You ought to be ashamed of yourself,
Will Anneys!" And Brune put his sister
gently behind him, and then marched
squarely up to his brother's face. "You
are as passionate as a brute beast, Will,
and that, too, with a poor little lass that
has her own troubles, and has borne

them like — like a good woman always does."

" I do not want to hear you speak, Brune."

"Ay, but I will speak, and you shall hear me. I tell you, Aspatria is in no kind to blame. The man came on her sudden, out of the plantation. She did not take his hand, she did not listen to him. She sent him about his business as quick as might be."

"Lottie Patterson saw her," said Will, dourly.

" Because Aspatria called Lottie Patterson to her; and if Lottie Patterson says she saw anything more or worse than ought to be, I will pretty soon call upon Seth Patterson to make his sister's words good. Cush! I will that! And what is more, Will Anneys, if you do not know how to take care of your sister's good name, I will teach you, — you mouse of a man! You go and side with that Frostham set against Aspatria! Chaff on the Frosthams! It is a bad neighbourhood where a girl like Aspatria cannot say a word or two on the king's highway at broad noonday, without having a *sisserara* about it."

" I did not side with the Frosthams against Aspatria."

" I 'll be bound you did ! "

" Let me alone, Brune ! Go your ways out of here, both of you ! "

" To be sure, we will both go. Come, Aspatria. When you are tired of ballooning, William Anneys, and can come down to common justice, maybe then I will talk to you, — not till."

Now, good honest anger is one of the sinews of the soul; and he that wants it when there is occasion has but a maimed mind. The hot words, the passionate atmosphere, the rebellion of Aspatria, the decision of Brune, had the same effect upon Will's senseless anger as a thunderstorm has upon the hot, heavy, summer air. Will raged his bad temper away, and was cool and clear-minded after it.

At the same hour the same kind of mental thunder-storm was prevailing over

all common-sense at Redware Hall. Ulfar,
after a long and vain watch for another
opportunity to speak to Aspatria, returned
there in a temper compounded of anger,
jealousy, disappointment, and unsatisfied
affection. He heard Lady Redware's
story of his own danger
and of Brune's considera-
tion with scornful indifference. Brune's consid-
eration he laughed at.
He knew very well, he
answered, that Brune
Anneys hated him, and
would take the greatest
delight in such a hubbub
as he pretended was in
project.

"But he came to please
Aspatria," continued Lady
Redware. "He said he came only to
please Aspatria."

"So Aspatria wishes me to leave Allerdale? I will not go."

"Sarah, he will not go," cried Lady

Redware, as her friend entered the room.
" He says he will not go."

" That is because you have appealed to
Ulfar's feelings instead of to his judgment.
When Ulfar considers how savagely primitive these dalesmen are in their passions,
he will understand that discretion is the
nobler part of valour. In Russia he
thought it a very prudent thing to get out
of the way when a pack of wolves were in
the neighbourhood."

" The law will protect me in this house.
Human beings have to mind the law."

" There are times when human beings
are a law unto themselves. How would
you like to see a crowd of angry men
shouting around this house for you?
Think of your sister, — and of me, if I am
worth so much consideration."

" I am not to be frightened, Sarah."

" Will you consider, then, that as far as
Keswick and Kendal on one side, and as
far as Dalton and Whitehaven on the other
side, every local newspaper will have, or
will make, its own version of the affair?

The Earl of Lonsdale, with a large party, is now at Whitehaven Castle. What a *sauce piquante* it will be to his dinners! How the men will howl over it, and how the women will snicker and smile !'"

"Sarah! you can think of the hatefullest things."

"And Lonsdale will go up to London purposely to have the delight of telling it at the clubs."

"Sarah !"

"And the 'Daily Whisper' will get Lonsdale's most delectable version, and blow it with the four winds of heaven to the four corners of the civilized world."

"Sarah Sandys, I — "

"Worse still! that poor girl whom you treated so abominably, must suffer the whole thing over again. Her name will be put as the head and front of your offending. All her sorrows and heartbreak will be made a penny mouthful for country bumpkins and scandalous gammers to 'Oh!' and 'Ah!' over. Ulfar, if you are a man, you will not give her a moment's

terror of such consequences. You may
see that she fears them, by her sending her
brother to entreat your absence."

"And I must be called coward and
runaway!"

"Let them call you anything they like,
so that you spare her further shame and
sorrow."

"Your talking in this fashion to me,
Sarah, is very like Satan correcting sin.
I loved Aspatria when I met you in
Rome."

"Of course! Adam always has his Eve
ready. 'Not my fault, good people!
Look at this woman! With her bright
smiles and her soft tongue she beguiled
me; and so I fell!' We can settle that
question, you and I, again. Now you
must ring the bell, and order your horse
— say, at four o'clock to-morrow morning.
You can have nearly six hours' sleep, —
quite enough for you."

"You have not convinced me, Sarah."

"Then you must ride now, and be convinced afterward. For your sister's sake

and for Aspatria's sake, you will surely go away."

Lady Redware was crying, and she cried a little harder to emphasize Sarah's pleading. Ulfar was in a hard strait. He looked angrily at the handsome little woman urging him to do the thing he hated to do, and then taking the kerchief from his sister's face, he kissed her, and promised to leave Redware at dawn of day.

"But," said he, "if you send me away now, I tell you, our parting is likely to be for many years, perhaps for life. I am going beyond civilization, and so beyond scandal."

"Do not flatter yourself so extravagantly, Ulfar. There is scandal everywhere, and always has been, even from the beginning. I have no doubt those nameless little sisters of Cain and Abel were talked about unpleasantly by their sisters and brothers-in-law. In fact, wherever there are women there are men glad to pull them down to their own level."

"Is it not very hard, then, that I am not to be permitted to stay here and defend the women I love?"

Sarah shook her head. "It is beyond your power, Ulfar. If Porthos were on earth again, or Amadis of Gaul, they might have happy and useful careers in handling as they deserve the maligners of good, quiet women. But the men of this era! — which of them durst lift the stone that the hand without sin is permitted to cast?"

So they talked the night away, drifting gradually from the unpleasant initial subject to Ulfar's plan of travel and

the far-off prospect of his return.   And in
the gray, cold dawn he bade them farewell,
and they watched him until he vanished in
the mists rolling down the mountain.   Then
they kissed each other, — a little, sad kiss
of congratulation, wet with tears; they had
won their desire, but their victory had left
them weeping.   Alas! it is the very condition of success that every triumph must be
baptized with somebody's tears.

This event, beginning in such a trifle as
an almost accidental visit of Aspatria to
the vicar, was the line sharply dividing
very different lives.   Nothing in Seat-
Ambar was ever quite the same after it.
William Anneys, indeed, quickly perceived
and acknowledged his fault, and the reconciliation was kind and complete; but Aspatria had taken a step forward, and crossed
clearly that bound which divides girlhood
from womanhood.   Unconsciously she assumed a carriage that Will felt compelled
to respect, and a tone was in her voice he
did not care to bluff and contradict.   He
never again ordered her to remain silent or

to leave his presence. A portion of his
household authority had passed from him,
both as regarded Aspatria and Brune; and
he felt himself to be less master than he
had formerly been.

Perhaps this was one reason of the growing frequency of his visits to Frostham.
There he was made much of, deferred to,
and all his little fancies flattered and
obeyed. Will knew he was the most important person in the world to Alice
Frostham; and he knew, also, that he
only shared Aspatria's heart with Ulfar
Fenwick. Men like the whole heart, and
nothing less than the whole heart; hence
Alice's influence grew steadily all through
the summer days, full to the brim of happy
labour and reasonable love. As early as
the haymaking Will told Aspatria that
Alice was coming to Seat-Ambar as its
mistress; and when the harvest was gathered in, the wedding took place. It was
as noisily jocund an affair as Aspatria's
had been silent and sorrowful; and Alice
Frostham, encircled by Will's protecting

arm, was led across the threshold of her
own new home, to the sound of music and
rejoicing.

The home was quickly divided, though
without unkind intent. Will and Alice had
their own talk, their own hopes and plans,
and Aspatria and Brune generally felt that
their entrance interfered with some discussion. So Aspatria and Brune began to
sit a great deal in Aspatria's room, and by
and by to discuss, in a confidential way,
what they were to do with their future.
Brune had no definite idea. Aspatria's
intents were clear and certain. But she
knew that she must wait until the spring
brought her majority and her freedom.

One frosty day, near Christmas, as Brune
was returning from Dalton, he heard himself called in a loud, cheerful voice. He
was passing Seat-Ketel, and he soon saw
Harry Ketel coming quickly toward him.
Harry wore a splendid scarlet uniform; and
the white snow beneath his feet, and the
dark green pines between which he walked,
made it all the more splendid by their

contrast. Brune had not seen Harry for five years; but they had been companions through their boyhood, and their memories were stored with the pleasant hours they had spent together.

Brune passed that night, and many subsequent ones, with his old friend; and when Harry went back to his regiment he took with him a certainty that Brune would soon follow. In fact, Harry had found his old companion in that mood which is ready to accept the first opening as the gift of fate. Brune found there was a commission to be bought in the Household Foot-Guards, and he was well able to pay for it. Indeed, Brune was by no means a poor man; his father had left him seven thousand pounds, and his share of the farm's proceeds had been constantly added to it.

Aspatria was delighted. She might now go to London in Brune's care. They discussed the matter constantly, and began to make the preparations necessary for the change. But affairs were not then ar-

ranged by steam and electricity, and the
letters relating to the purchase and transfer of Brune's commission occupied some
months in their transit to and fro; although
Brune did not rely upon the postman's
idea of the practicability of the roads.

Aspatria's correspondence was also uncertain and unsatisfactory for some time.
She had at first no guide to a school but
the advertisements in the London papers
which Harry sent to his friend. But one
night Brune, without any special intention,
named the matter to Mrs. Ketel; and that
lady was able to direct Aspatria to an
excellent school in Richmond, near London. And as she was much more favour-
ably situated for a quick settlement of
the affair, she undertook the necessary
correspondence.

Will was not ignorant of these movements, but Alice induced him to be passive
in them. "No one can then blame us,
Will, whatever happens." And as Will
and Alice were extremely sensitive to
public opinion, this was a good consid-

eration. Besides Alice, not unnaturally, wished to have the Seat to herself; so that Aspatria's and Brune's wishes fitted admirably into her own desires, and it gave her a kind of selfish pleasure to forward them.

The ninth of March was Aspatria's twenty-first birthday; and it was to her a very important anniversary, for she received as its gift her freedom and her fortune. There was no hitch or trouble in its transfer from Will to herself. Honour and integrity were in the life-blood of William Anneys, honesty and justice the very breath of his nostrils. Aspatria's fortune had been guarded with a super-sensitive care; and when years gave her its management, Will surrendered it cheerfully to her control.

Fortunately, the school selected by Mrs. Ketel satisfied Will thoroughly; and Brune's commission in the Foot-Guards was in honourable accord with the highest traditions and spirit of the dales. For the gigantic and physically handsome men of

these mountain valleys have been for centuries considered the finest material for
those regiments whose duty it is to guard

the
persons
and the
homes of
royalty. Brune
had only followed   in the
steps of a great num-   ber of his
ancestors.

In the beginning of   ·   April, Aspatria left Seat-Ambar for London, — left
forever all the pettiness of her house life,
chairs and tables, sewing and meals, and
the useless daily labour that has to be continually done over again.   And at the last
Will was very tender with her, and even
Alice did her best to make the parting

days full of hope and kindness. As for the journey, there was no anxiety; Brune was to travel with his sister, and see her safely within her new home.

Yet neither of them left the old home without some tears. Would they ever see again those great, steadfast hills, that purify those who walk upon them; ever dwell again within the dear old house, that had not been builded, but had grown with the family it had sheltered, through a thousand years? They hardly spoke to each other, as they drove through the sweet valleys, where the sunshine laid a gold on the green, and the warm south-wind gently rocked the daisies, and the lark's song was like a silvery water-fall up in the sky.

But they were young; and, oh, the rich significance of the word " young " when the heart is young as well as the body, when the thoughts are not doubts, and when the eyes look not backward, but only forward, into a bright future !

CHAPTER VI.

"LOVE SHALL BE LORD OF SANDY-SIDE."

DURING thirty years of the first half of
this century Mrs. St. Alban's finishing
school for young gentlewomen was a
famous institution of its kind. For she
had been born to the manner of courts
and of people of high degree; and when
evil fortune met her, she very wisely
turned her inherited social advantages into
a means of honest livelihood. Aspatria
was much impressed by her noble bearing
and fine manners, and by the elaborate
state in which the twelve pupils, of whom
she was one, lived.

Each had her own suite of apartments;
each was expected to keep a maid, and to
dress with the utmost care and propriety.
There were fine horses in the stables for
their equestrian exercise, there were grooms

to attend them during it, and there were
regular reception-days, which afforded
tyros in social accomplishments practical
opportunities for cultivating the graceful
and gracious urbanity which evidences
really fine breeding.

Many of Aspatria's companions were of
high rank, — Lady Julias and Lady Augus-
tas, who were destined to wear ducal
coronets and to stand around the throne
of their young queen. But they were
always charmingly pleasant and polite,
and Aspatria soon acquired their outward
form of calm deliberation and their mode
of low, soft speech. For the rest, she
decided, with singular prudence, to culti-
vate only those talents which nature had
obviously granted her.

A few efforts proved that she had no
taste for art. Indeed, the attempt to por-
tray the majesty of the mountains or the
immensity of the ocean seemed to her
childishly petty and futile. She had dwelt
among the high places and been familiar
with the great sea, and to make images of

them appeared a kind of sacrilege. But she liked the study of languages, and she had a rich contralto voice capable of expressing all the emotions of the heart. At the piano she hesitated; its music, under her unskilled fingers, sounded mechanical; she doubted her ability to put a soul into that instrument. But the harp was different; its strings held sympathetic tones she felt competent to master. To these studies she added a course of English literature and dancing. She was already a fine rider, and her information obtained from the vicar's library and the Encyclopædia covered an enormous variety of subjects, though it was desultory, and in many respects imperfect.

Her new life was delightful to her. She had an innate love for study, for quiet, and for elegant surroundings. These tastes were fully gratified. The large house stood in a fair garden, surrounded by very high walls, with entrance-gates of handsomely wrought iron. Perfect quiet reigned within this flowery enclosure. She could study

without the constant interruptions which
had annoyed her at home; and she was
wisely aided in her studies by masters

whose low
voices and glid-
ing steps seemed
only to accentuate the
peace of the wide school-
room, with its perfect appoint-
ments and its placid group of
beautiful students.

On Saturdays Brune gen-
erally spent several hours
with her; and if the weather
were fine, they rode or walked in the Park.
Brune was a constant wonder to Aspatria.
Certainly his handsome uniform had done
much for him, but there was a greater

change than could be effected by mere clothes. Without losing that freshness and singleness of mind he owed to his country training, he had become a man of fashion, a little of a dandy, a very innocent sort of a lady-killer. His arrival caused always a faint flutter in Mrs. St. Alban's dove-cot, and the noble damosels found many little womanly devices to excuse their passing through the parlour while Brune was present. They liked to see him bend his beautiful head to them; and Lady Mary Boleyn, who was Aspatria's friend and companion, was mildly envied the privileges this relation gave her.

During the vacations Aspatria was always the guest of one or other of her mates, though generally she spent them at the splendid seat of the Boleyns in Hampshire, and the unconscious education thus received was of the greatest value to her. It gave the ease of nature to acquired accomplishments, and, above all, that air which we call distinction, which is rarely natural, and is attained only by frequent association with those who dwell on the highest social peaks.

Much might be said of this phase of Aspatria's life which may be left to the reader's imagination. For three years it saw only such changes as advancing intelligence and growing friendships made. The real change was in Aspatria personally. No one could have traced without constant doubt the slim, virginal, unfinished-looking girl that left Scat-Ambar, in the womanly perfection of Aspatria aged twenty-four years. She had grown several inches taller; her angles had all disappeared; every joint was softly rounded. Her hands and arms were exquisite; her throat and the poise of her head like those of a Greek goddess. Her hair was darker and more abundant, and her eyes retained all their old charm, with some rarer and nobler addition.

To be sure, she had not the perfect regularity of feature that distinguished some of her associates, that exact beauty which Titian's Venus possesses, and which makes

no man's heart beat a throb the faster.
Her face had rather the mobile irregularity
of Leonardo's Mona Lisa, the charming
face that men love passionately, the face
that men can die for.

At the close of the third year she refused all invitations for the summer holi-
days, and went back to Seat-Ambar.
There had not been much communication
between Will and herself. He was occupied with his land and his sheep, his wife
and his two babies. People then took
each other's affection as a matter of course,
without the daily assurance of it. About
twice a year Will had sent her a few
strong words of love, and a bare descrip-
tion of any change about the home, or
else Alice had covered a sheet with pretty
nothings, written in the small, pointed,
flowing characters then fashionable.

But the love of Aspatria for her home
depended on no such trivial, accidental
tokens. It was in her blood ; her personality was knotted to Seat-Ambar by centuries of inherited affection ; she could test

it by the fact that it would have killed her
to see it pass into a stranger's hands. When
once she had turned her face northward,
it seemed impossible to travel quickly
enough. Hundreds of miles away she

felt the cool wind blowing through the
garden, and the scent of the damask rose
was on it. She heard the gurgling of
the becks and the wayside streams, and the
whistling of the boys in the barn, and the
tinkling of the sheep-bells on the highest
fells. The raspberries were ripe in their
sunny corner; she tasted them afar off.

The dark oak rooms, their perfume of ancient things, their air of homelike comfort, — it was all so vivid, so present to her memory, that her heart beat and thrilled, as the breast of a nursing mother thrills and beats for her longing babe.

She had told no one she was coming; for, the determination made, she knew that she would reach home before the Dalton postman got the letter to Seat-Ambar. The gig she had hired she left at the lower garden gate; and then she walked quickly through the rose-alley up to the front door. It stood open, and she heard a baby crying. How strange the wailing notes sounded! She went forward, and opened the parlour door; Alice was washing the child, and she turned with an annoyed look to see the intruder.

Of course the expression changed, but not quickly enough to prevent Aspatria seeing that her visit was inopportune. Alice said afterward that she did not recognize her sister-in-law, and, as Will met her

precisely as he would have met an entire
stranger, Alice's excuse was doubtless a
valid one.   There were abundant exclama-
tions and rejoicings when her identity was
established, but Will could do nothing all
the evening but wonder over the changes
that had taken place in his sister.

However, when the first joy of reunion
is over, it is a prudent thing not to try too
far the welcome that is given to the home-
comer who has once left home.   Will and
Alice had grown to the idea that Aspatria would never return to claim the room
in Seat-Ambar which was hers legally so
long as she lived.   It had been refurnished
and was used as a guest-room.   Aspatria
looked with dismay on the changes made.
Her very sampler had been sent away, —
the bit of canvas made sacred by her
mother's fingers holding her own over it.
She could remember the instances con-
nected with the formation of almost every
letter of its simple prayer, —

> Jesus, permit thy gracious name to stand
> As the first effort of my infant hand ;

And, as my fingers on the sampler move,
Engage my tender heart to seek thy love.
With thy dear children may I have a part,
And write thy Name, thyself, upon my heart.

And it was gone! She went into the
lumber-room, and picked it out from under
a pile of old prints and shabbily framed
certificates for prize cattle.

With a sad heart Aspatria regarded the
other changes. Her little tent-bed, with
its white dimity curtains, had been given
to baby's nurse. The vase her father had
bought her at Kendal fair was broken.
Her small mirror and dressing-table had
been removed for a fine Psyche in a
gilded frame. Nothing, nothing was un-
touched, but the big dower-chest into
which she had flung her wretched wedding-
clothes. She stood silently before it,
reflecting, with excusable ill-nature, that
neither Will nor Alice knew the secret of
its spring. Her mother had taught it to
her, and that bit of knowledge she determined to keep to herself.

After some hesitation she tried the

spring: it answered her pressure at once;
the lid flew back, and there lay the unhappy white satin dress, the wreath, and

veil, and slippers, just as she had tumbled
them in. The bitter hour came sharply
back to her; she thought and gazed, and
thought and gazed, until she felt herself
to be weeping. Then she softly closed

the lid, and, as she did so, a smile parted
her lips, — a smile that denied all that her
tears said; a smile of hope, of good pres-
age, of coming happiness.

She stayed only a week at Seat-Ambar,
though she had originally intended to
remain until the harvest was over. The
time was spent in public festivity; every
one in Allerdale was invited to give her a
fitting welcome. But the very formality
of all this entertainment pained her. It
was, after all, only a cruel evidence that
Will and Alice did not care to take her into
their real home-life. She would rather
have sat alone with them, and talked of
their hopes and plans, and been permitted
to make friends of the babies.

So far away, so far away as she had
drifted in three years from the absent living! Would the dead be kinder? She
went to Aspatria Church and sat down in
her mother's seat, and let the strange spir-
itual atmosphere which hovers in old
churches fill her heart with its supernatural
influence. All around her were the graves

of her
fore-elders,
strong elemen-
tal men, simple
God-loving women.
Did they know her?
Did they care for her?
Her soul looked with
piteous entreaty into the void behind it,
but there was no answer; only that dread-
ful silence of the dead, which presses upon
the drum of the ear like thunder.

She went into the quiet yard around the

church. The ancient, ancient sun shone
on the young grass. Over her mother's
grave the sweet thyme had grown luxuri-
antly. She rubbed her hands in it, and
spread them toward heaven with a prayer.
Then peace came into her heart, and she
felt as if eyes, unseen heavenly eyes,
rained happy influence upon her. Thus
it is that death imparts to life its most
intense interest; for, kneeling in his very
presence, Aspatria forgot the mortality of
her parents, and did reverence to that
within them which was eternal.

She returned to London, and was a little
disappointed there also. Mrs. St. Alban
had promised herself an absolute release
from any outside element. She felt Aspatria a trifle in the way, and, though far
too polite to show her annoyance, Aspatria by some similar instinct divined it.
That is the way always. When we plan
for ourselves, all our plans fail. Happy
are they who learn early to let fate alone,
and never interfere with the Powers who
hold the thread of their destiny!

It was not until she had reached this mood, a kind of content indifference, that her good genius could work for her. She then sent Brune as her messenger, and Brune took his sister to meet her on Richmond Hill. On their way thither they talked about Seat-Ambar, and Will and Alice, until Aspatria suddenly noticed that Brune was not listening to her. His eyes were fixed upon a lovely woman approaching them. It was Sarah Sandys. Brune stood bareheaded to receive her salutation.

"I never should have known you, Lieutenant Anneys," she said, extending her hand, and beaming like sunshine on the handsome officer, "had not your colonel Jardine been in Richmond to-day. He is very proud of you, sir, and said so many fine things of you that I am ambitious to show him that we are old acquaintances. May I know, through you, Mrs. Anneys also?"

"This is my sister, Mrs. Sandys, — my sister—" Brune hesitated a moment, and then said firmly, "Miss Anneys."

Then Sarah insisted on taking them to her house to lunch; and there she soon had them under her influence. She waited on them with ravishing smiles and all sorts of pretty offices. She took them in her handsome carriage to drive, she insisted on their remaining to dinner. And before the drive was over, she had induced Aspatria to extend her visit until the opening of Mrs. St. Alban's school.

"We three are from the north country," she said, with an air of relationship; "and how absurd for Miss Anneys to be alone at Mrs. St. Alban's, where she is not wanted, and for me to be alone here, when I desire her society so much!"

Aspatria was much pleased to receive such a delightful invitation, and a messenger was sent at once for her maid. Mrs. St. Alban was quite ready to resign Aspatria, and the maid was as glad as her mistress to leave the lonely mansion. In an hour or two she had removed Aspatria's wardrobe, and was arranging the pleasant rooms Mrs. Sandys had placed at her guest's disposal.

Sarah was evidently bent on conquest.
Her toilet was a marvellous combination
of some shining blue and white texture,
mingled with pink roses and gold ornaments. Her soft fair
hair was loosened
and curled, and she
had a childlike man-
ner of being care-
lessly happy. Brune
sat at her right hand;
she talked to him in
smiles and glances,
and gave her words
to Aspatria. She
was determined to
please both sister
and brother, and she
succeeded. Aspatria
thought she had
never in all her life seen a woman so lovable, so amusing, so individual.

Brune was naturally shy and silent
among women. Sarah made him elo-
quent, because she had the tact to dis-

cover the subject on which he could talk,— his regiment, and its sayings and doings. So Brune was delighted with himself; he had never before suspected how clever he was. Stimulated by Sarah's and Aspatria's laughter and curiosity, he found it easy to retail funny little bits of palace and mess gossip, and to describe the queer men and the vain men and the fine fellows that were his familiars.

" And pray how do you amuse yourself, Lieutenant? Do you drink wine, and gamble, and go to the races, and bet your purse empty?"

" I was never brought up in such ways," Brune answered, " and, I can tell you, I would n't make believe to like them. There are a good many dalesmen in my company, and none of us enjoy anything more than a fair throw or an in-lock."

" A throw or an in-lock! What do you mean, Lieutenant ? You must explain yourself to Miss Anneys and myself."

" Aspatria knows well enough. Did you ever see north-country lads wrestling,

madam? No? Then you have as fine a
thing in keeping for your eyes as human
creatures can show you. I 'll warrant that!
Why-a! wrestling brings all men to their
level. When Colonel Jardine is ugly-tem-
pered, and top-heavy with his authority, a
few sound throws over Timothy Sutcliffe's
head does bring him to level very well. I
had a little in-play with him yesterday;
for in the wrestling-ring we be all equals,
though out of it he is my colonel."

" Now for the in-play. Tell me about
it, for I see Miss Anneys is not at all
interested."

" Colonel Jardine is a fine wrestler; a
fair match he would be even for brother
Will. Yesterday he said he could throw
me; and I took the challenge willingly.
So we shook hands, and went squarely for
the throw. I was in good luck, and soon
got my head under his right arm, and his
head close down to my left side. Then it
was only to get my right arm up to his
shoulder, and lift him as high as my head,
and, when so, lean backward and throw

him over my head: we call it the Flying Horse."

" Oh, I can see it very well.   No wonder Rosalind fell in love with Orlando when he threw the wrestler Charles."

"Were they north-country or Cornish men?"

She was far too kindly and polite to smile; indeed, she gave Aspatria a pretty, imperative glance, and answered, in the most natural manner, " I think they were Italians."

" Oh!" said Brune, with some contempt. "Chaff on their ways!   The Devonshire wrestlers are brutal; the Cornish are too slow; but the Cumberland men wrestle like gentlemen.   They meet square and level in the ring, and the one who could carry ill-will for a fair throw would very soon find himself out of all rings and all good fellowship."

"You said ' even brother Will.'   Is your brother a better wrestler than you?"

"My song! he is that!   Will has his match, though.   We had a ploughman

once, — Aspatria remembers him, — Robert
Steadman, an upright, muscular young
fellow, civil and respectful as could be in
everything about his work and place; but
on wet days when we were all, masters and
servants, in the barn together, it was a
sight to see Robert wrestling with Will for
the mastery, and Will never so ready to
say, 'Well done!' nor the rest of us so
happy, as when we saw Will's two brawny
legs going handsomely over Robert's
head."

" If I were a man, I should try to be a
fine wrestler."

" It is a great comfort," said Brune.
" If you have a quarrel of any kind, it is a
deal more satisfactory to meet your man,
and throw him a few times over your head,
than to go to law with him. It puts a
stop to unpleasantness very quickly and
very good-naturedly."

Then Sarah rose and opened the piano,
and from its keys dashed out a lilting,
hurrying melody, like the galloping of
horses and shaking of bridles; and in a

few moments she began to sing, and Brune
went to her side, and, because she looked
so steadily into his eyes, he could remember nothing at all of the song but its
dashing refrain, —

> "For he whom I wed
>   Must be north country bred,
> And must carry me back to the North Countrie."

Then Aspatria played some wonderful
music on her harp, and Sarah and Brune
sat still and listened to their own hearts,
and sent out shy glances, and caught
each other in the act, and Brune was
made nervous, and Sarah gay, by the
circumstance.

By and by they began to talk of schools,
and of how much Aspatria had learned;
and so Brune regretted his own ignorance,
and wished he had been more attentive to
his schoolmaster.

Sarah laughed at the wish. "A knowledge of Shakspeare and the musical
glasses and the Della Cruscans," she said,
"is for foolish, sentimental women. You
can wrestle, and you can fight, and I

suppose you can make money, and perhaps even make love. Is there anything
else a soldier needs? "

"Colonel Jardine is very clever," continued Brune, regretfully; "and I had a
good schoolmaster — "

"Nonsense, Lieutenant!" said Sarah.
"None of them are good. They all spoil
your eyes, and seek to lay a curse on you;
that is the confusion of languages."

"Still, I might have learned Latin."

"It was the speech of pagans and
infidels."

"Or logic."

"Logic hath nothing to say in a good
cause."

"Or philosophy."

"Philosophy is curiosity. Socrates was
very properly put to death for it."

They were all laughing together, when
Sarah condemned Socrates, and the evening passed like a happy dream away.

It was succeeded by weeks of the same
delight. Aspatria soon learned to love
Sarah. She had never before had a

woman friend on whom she could rely
and to whom she could open her heart.
Sarah induced her to speak of Ulfar, to
tell her all her suffering and her plans and
hopes, and she gave her in return a true
affection and a most sincere sympathy.
Nothing of the past that referred to Ulfar
was left untold; and as the two women sat
together during the long summer days,
they grew very near to each other, and
there was but one mind and one desire
between them.

So that when the time came for Aspatria
to go back to Mrs. St. Alban's, Sarah
would not hear of their separation. "You
have had enough of book-learning," she
said. "Remain with me. We will go to
Paris, to Rome, to Vienna. We will study
through travel and society. It is by rub-
bing yourself against all kinds of men and
women that you acquire the finest polish
of life; and then when Ulfar comes back
you will be able to meet him upon all
civilized grounds. And as for the South
Americans, we will buy all the books

about them we can find. Are they red
or white or black, I wonder? Are they
pagans or Christians? I seem to remember that when I was at school I
learned that the Peruvians worshipped
the sun."

"I think, Sarah, that they are all descen-
dants of Spaniards; so they must be
Roman Catholics. And I have read that
their women are beautiful and witty."

"My dear Aspatria, nothing goes with
Spaniards but gravity and green olives."

Aspatria was easily persuaded to accept
Sarah's offer; she was indeed very happy
in the prospect before her. But Brune was
miserable. He had spent a rapturous
summer, and it was to end without harvest, or the promise thereof. He could
not endure the prospect, and one night he
made a movement so decided that Sarah
was compelled to set him back a little.

"Were you ever in love, Mrs. Sandys?"
poor Brune asked, with his heart filling his
mouth.

She looked thoughtfully at him a moment, and then slowly answered: "I once felt myself in danger, and I fled to France. I consider it the finest action of my life."

Aspatria felt sorry for her brother, and she said warmly: "I think no one falls in love now. Love is out of date."

Sarah enjoyed her temper. "You are right, dear," she answered. "Culture makes love a conscious operation. When women are all feeling, they fall in love; when they have intellect and will, they attach themselves only after a critical examination of the object."

Later, when they were alone, Aspatria took her friend to task for her cruelty: "You know Brune loves you, Sarah; and you do love him. Why make him miserable? Has he presumed too far?"

"No, indeed! He is as adoring and humble as one could wish a future lord and master to be."

"Well, then?"

"I will give our love time to grow. When we come back, if Brune has been true to me in every way, he may fall to blessing himself with both hands;" and then she began to sing, —

"Betide, betide, whatever betide,
Love shall be Lord of Sandy-Side!"

"Love is a burden two hearts carry very easily together, but, oh, Sarah! I know how hard it is to bear it alone. Therefore I say, be kind to Brune while you can."

"My dear, your idea is a very pretty one. I read the other day a Hindu version of it that smelled charmingly of the soil, —

'A clapping is not made with one hand alone :
Your love, my beloved, must answer my own.'"

But in spite of such reflections, Sarah's will and intellect were predominant, and she left poor Brune with only such hope as he could glean from the lingering pressure of her hand and the tears in her eyes. Aspatria's pleading had done no good. Perhaps it had done harm; for the very nature of love is that it should be spontaneous.

CHAPTER VII.

"A ROSE OF A HUNDRED LEAVES."

ONE morning in spring Aspatria stood in a balcony overlooking the principal thoroughfare of Rome,—the Rome of papal government, mythical, mystical, mediæval in its character. A procession of friars had just passed; a handsome boy was crying violets; some musical puppets were performing in the shadow of the opposite palace; a party of brigands were going to the Angelo prison; the spirit of Cæsar was still abroad in the black-browed men and women, lounging and laughing in their gaudy, picturesque costumes; and the spirit of ecclesiasticism lifted itself above every earthly object, and touched proudly the bells of a thousand churches. Aspatria was weary of all.

She had that morning an imperative nostalgia. She could see nothing but the

mountains of Cumberland, and the white
sheep wandering about their green sides.
Through the church-
bells she heard the
sheep-bells.
Above the boy
crying violets
she heard the
boy whistling
in the fresh-
ploughed furrow.
As for the vio-
lets, she knew
how the wild
ones were blow-
ing in Ambar
wood, and how
in the garden the
daffodil-beds were aglow,
and the sweet thyme hum-
bling itself at their feet, because each bore a chalice. Oh for a
breath from the mountains and the sea!
The hot Roman streets, with their ever-
changing human elements of sorrow and

mirth, sin and prayer, riches and poverty, made her sad and weary.

Sarah came toward her with a letter in her hand. "Ria," she said, "this is from Lady Redware. Your husband will be in England very shortly."

It was the first time Sarah had ever called Ulfar Aspatria's husband. In conversation the two women had always spoken of him as "Ulfar." The change was significant. It implied that Sarah thought the time had come for Aspatria to act decisively.

"I shall be delighted to go back to England. We have been twenty months away, Sarah. I was just feeling as if it were twenty years."

Sarah looked critically at the woman who was going to cast her last die for love. She was so entirely different from the girl who had first won that love, how was it possible for her to recapture the same sweet, faithless emotion? She had a swift memory of the slim girl in the plain black frock whom she had seen sitting under the

whin-bushes. And then she glanced at
Aspatria standing under the blue-and-red
awning of the Roman palace. She was
now twenty-six years old, and in the very
glory of her womanhood, tall, superbly
formed, graceful, calm, and benignant.
Her face was luminous with intellect and
feeling, her manner that of a woman high-
bred and familiar with the world. Culture
had done all for her that the lapidary does
for the diamond; travel and social advantages had added to the gem a golden setting. She was so little like the sorrowful
child whom Ulfar had last seen in the
vicar's meadow that Sarah felt instantaneous recognition to be almost impossible.

After some hesitation, Aspatria agreed
to accept Sarah's plan and wait in Richmond the development of events. At first
she had been strongly in favour of a
return to Seat-Ambar. "If Ulfar really
wants to see me," she said, "he will be
most likely to seek me there."

"But then, Ria, he may think he does
not want to see you. Men never know

what they really do want. You have to give them ‘ leadings.’ If Ulfar can look on you now and have no curiosity about your identity, I should say the man was not worth a speculation from any point. See if you have hold sufficient on his memory to pique his curiosity. If you have, lead him wherever you wish."

" But how? And where?"

" Do I carry a divining-cup, Ria? Can I foresee the probabilities of a man so impossible as Ulfar Fenwick? I only know that Richmond is a good place to watch events from."

And of course the Richmond house suited Brune. His love had grown to the utmost of Sarah's expectations, and he was no longer to be put off with smiles and pleasant words. Sarah had promised him an answer when she returned, and he claimed it with a passionate persistence that had finally something imperative in it. To this mood Sarah succumbed; though she declared that Brune had chosen the morning of all others most inconvenient

for her. She was just leaving the house.
She was going to London about her
jewels. Brune had arrested the coachman
by a peremptory movement, and he looked
as if he were quite prepared to lift Sarah
out of the carriage.

So Aspatria went alone. She was glad
of the swift movement in the fresh air, she
was glad that she could be quiet and let
it blow passively upon her. The restless-
ness of watching had made her feverish.
She had the "strait" of a strong mind
which longs to meet her destiny. For her
love for her husband had grown steadily
with her efforts to be worthy of that love,
and she longed to meet him face to face
and try the power of her personality over
him. The trial did not frighten her; she
felt within her the ability to accomplish
it; her feet were on a level with her task;
she was the height of a woman above
it.

Musing on this subject, letting her mind
shoot to and fro like a shuttle between the
past and the present, she reached Picca-

dilly, and entered a large jeweller's shop.
The proprietor was talking to a gentleman
who was exhibiting a number of uncut
gems. Aspatria knew him instantly. It
was Ulfar Fenwick,— the same Ulfar, older,
and yet distinctly handsomer. For the
dark hair slightly whitened, and the thin,
worn cheeks, had an intensely human
aspect. She saw that he had suffered;
that the sum of life was on his face, — toil,
difficulty, endurance, mind, and also that
pathetic sadness which tells of endurance
without avail.

She went to the extreme end of the
counter, and began to examine the jewels
which Sarah had sent to be reset. Some
were finished ; others were waiting for the
selection of a particular style, and Aspatria
looked critically at the models shown her.
The occupation gave her an opportunity
to calm and consider herself ; she could
look at the jewels a few moments without
expressing an opinion.

Then she gave, in a clear, distinct voice,
some order regarding a pearl necklace ;

and Ulfar turned like a flash, and looked
at the woman who had spoken. She had
the pearls in one hand; the other touched
a satin cushion on which lay many ornaments of diamonds, sapphires, and rubies.
The moonlight iridescence of the pearls,
the sparkling glory of the gems, seemed
to be a part of her noble beauty. He
forgot his own treasures, and stood looking at the woman whose voice had called
to him out of the past, had penetrated his
heart like a bell struck sharply in its innermost room. Who was it? Where had
they met before? He knew the face. He
knew, and yet he did not know, the whole
charming personality. As she turned,
his eyes met her eyes, and the pure pallor
of her cheeks was flooded with crimson.

She passed him within touch; the rustle
of her garments, their faint perfume, the
simple sense of her nearness, thrilled his
being wondrously. And, above all, that
sense of familiarity! What could it mean?
He gave the stones into the jeweller's care,
and hurriedly followed her steps.

"That is Sarah Sandys's carriage, my barony for it!" he exclaimed; "and the men are in the Sandys livery. Sarah, then, is in Richmond; and the woman who rides in her carriage is very likely in her house; but who can it be?"

The face haunted him, the voice tormented him like a melody that we continually try to catch. He endeavoured to place both as he rode out to Richmond. More than once the thought of Aspatria came to him, but he could not make any memory of her fit that splendid vision of the woman with uplifted hand and the string of pearls dropping from it. Her exquisite face, between the beauty of their reflection and the flashing of the gems beneath, retained in his memory a kind of glory. "Such loveliness is the proper setting for pearls and diamonds," he said. "Many a beauty I have seen, but none that can touch the heel of her shoe."

For he really thought that it was her personal charms which had so moved him. It was the sense of familiarity; it was in a far deeper and dimmer way a presentiment of right, of possession, a feeling of personal touch in the emotion, which perplexed and stimulated him as the mere mystery and beauty of the flesh could never have done.

As soon as he reached the top of Richmond Hill he saw Sarah. She was sauntering along that loveliest of cliffs, with Brune. An orderly was leading Brune's horse; he himself was in the first ecstasy of Sarah's acknowledged love. Ulfar went into the Star and Garter Inn and watched Sarah. He had no claim upon her, and yet he felt as if she had been false to him. "And for a mere soldier!" Then he looked critically at the soldier, and said,

with some contempt: "I am sorry for him! Sarah Sandys will have her pastime, and then say, 'Farewell, good sir!'" As for the mere soldier being Brune Anneys, that was a thought out of Ulfar's horizon.

In a couple of hours he went to Sarah's. She met him with real delight.

"You are just five years lovelier, Sarah," he said.

"Admiration from Sir Ulfar Fenwick is admiration indeed!"

"Yes; I say you are beautiful, though I have just seen the most bewitching woman that ever blessed my eyes,—in your carriage too." And then, swift as light or thought, there flashed across his mind a conviction that the Beauty and Aspatria were identical. It was a momentary intelligence; he grasped it merely as a clew that might lead him somewhere.

"In my carriage? I dare say it was Ria. She went to Piccadilly this morning about some jewels."

"She reminded me of Aspatria."

"Have you brought back with you that

old trouble? I have no mind to hear
more of it."

"Who is the lady I saw this morning?"

"She is the sister of the man I am going to marry. In four months she will be
my sister."

"What is her name?"

"That is to tell you my secret, sir."

"I saw you throwing your enchantments
over some soldier. I knew just how the
poor fellow felt."

"Then you also have been in Arcadia.
Be thankful for your past blessings. I do
not expect you to rejoice with me; none
of the apostolic precepts are so hard as
that which bids us rejoice with those who
do rejoice."

"Neither Elizabeth nor you have ever
named Aspatria in your letters."

"Did you expect us to change guard
over Ambar-Side? I dare say Aspatria
has grown into a buxom, rosy-cheeked
woman and quite forgotten you."

"I must go and see her."

"I think you ought. Also, you should

give her her freedom. I consider your
behaviour a dog-in-the-manger atrocity."

" Can you not pick nicer words, Sarah? "

" I would not if I could."

" Sarah, tell me truly, have I lost my
good looks? "

She regarded him attentively a moment,
and answered: " Not quite. You have
some good points yet. You have grown
thin and gray, and lost something, and
perhaps gained something; but you are
not very old, and then, you know, you
have your title, and your castle, and your
very old, old family, and I suppose a good
deal of money." In reality, she was sure
that he had never before been so attrac-
tive; for he had now the magic of a
countenance informed by intellect and
experience, eyes brimming with light, lips
neither loose nor coarse, yet full of passion
and the faculty of enjoyment.

He smiled grimly at Sarah's list of his
charms, and said, " When will you intro-
duce me to your future sister? "

" This evening. Come about nine. I

have a few sober people who will be delighted to hear your South American adventures. Ria goes to Lady Chester's ball soon after nine. Do not miss your chance."

" Could I see her now? "

" You could not."

" What for? "

" Do you suppose she would leave a *modiste* for — you? "

" I wonder where Aspatria is! "

" Go and find out."

" Sarah, who is the young lady I saw in your carriage? "

" She is the sister of the officer you saw me with, the man I am going to marry."

" Where did you meet him? "

" At a friend's house."

" Where did you meet her? "

" Her brother brought her to my house. I asked her to stay with me, and finally we went to Italy together."

" She has a very aristocratic manner."

" She ought to have. She was educated at Mrs. St. Alban's, and she visits at the

Earl of Arundel's, the Duke of Norfolk's,
and the very exclusive Boleyns', — Lady
Mary Boleyn is her friend, and she has
also had the great advantage of my society
for nearly two years."

"Then of course she is not Aspatria,
and my heart is a liar, and my memory is
a traitor, and my eyes do not see correctly.
I will call about nine. I am at the Star
and Garter. If she should name me at
all — "

"Do you imagine she noticed you? and
in such a public place as Howell's?"

"I really do imagine she noticed me.
Ask her."

"I see you are in love again. After all
that experience has done for you! It is a
Nemesis, Ulfar. I have often noticed that,
however faithless a man may be, there
comes at last one woman who avenges
all the rest. Enter Nemesis at nine
to-night!"

"Sarah, you are an angel."

"Thank you, Ulfar. I thought you
classed me with the other side."

" As for Aspatria — "

" Life is too short to discuss Aspatria. I remember one day at Redware being sharply requested to keep silence on that subject. The wheel of retribution has made a perfect circle as regards Aspatria! I shall certainly tell Ria that you have made her the heroine of your disagreeable matrimonial romance."

" No, no, Sarah! Do not say a word to her. I must wait until nine, I suppose? And I am so anxious and so fearful, Sarah."

" You must wait until nine. And as for the rest, I know very well that in the present age a lover's cares and fears have

Dwindled to the smallest span.

Do go to your hotel, and get clothed and in your right mind. You are most unbecomingly dressed. Good-by, old friend, good-by!" And she left him with an elaborate courtesy.

Ulfar was now in a vortex. Things went around and around in his conscious-

ness; and whenever he endeavoured to
examine events with his reason, then feeling advanced some unsupported conviction,
and threw him back into the same senseless whirl of emotion.

He had failed to catch
the point which would
have given him the clew
to the whole mystery,
— the identity of Brune
with the splendidly ac-
coutred officer Sarah
avowed to be her in-
tended husband.
Without taking special
note of him, Ulfar had
seen certain signs of birth,
breeding, and assured
position. In his mind
there was a great gulf
between the haughty-
looking soldier and
the simple, handsome, but rather boorish-
looking young Squire of Ambar-Side.
The two individualities were as far apart

in social claims as the north and south
poles are apart physically.

And if this beautiful woman were indeed
Aspatria, how could he reconcile the fact
with her education at St. Alban's, her
friendship with such exalted families, her
relationship to an officer of evident birth
and position? When he thought thus, he
acknowledged the impossibility; but then
no sooner had he acknowledged it than his
heart passionately denied the deduction,
with the simple iteration, "It is Aspatria!
It is Aspatria!"

Aspatria or not, he told himself that he
was at last genuinely in love. Every affair
before was tame, pale, uninteresting. If
it was not Aspatria, then the first Aspatria
was the shadow of the second and real one;
the preface to love's glorious tale; the pre-
lude to his song; the gray, sweet dawn to
his perfect day. He could not eat, nor sit
still, nor think reasonably, nor yet stop
thinking. The sun stood still; the minutes
were hours; at four o'clock he wished to
fling the timepiece out of the window.

Aspatria had the immense strength of certainty. She knew. Also, she had Sarah to advise with. Still better, she had the conviction that Ulfar loved her. Perhaps Sarah had exaggerated Ulfar's desperate condition; if so, she had done it consciously, for she knew that as soon as a woman is sure of her power she puts on an authority which commands it. She was now only afraid that Ulfar would not be kept in suspense long enough, that Aspatria would forgive him too easily.

"Do make yourself as puzzling as you can, for this one night, Aspatria," she urged. "Try to outvie and outdo and even affront that dove-like simplicity he used to adore in you, and into which you are still apt to relapse. He told me once that you looked like a Quakeress when he first saw you."

"I was just home from Miss Gilpin's school in Kendal. It was a Quaker school. I have always kept a black gown ready, like the one he saw me first in."

"No black gown to-night. I have a mind to stay here and see that you turn the Quakeress into a princess."

"I will do all you wish. To-night you shall have your way; but poor Ulfar must have suffered, and —"

"Poor Ulfar, indeed! Be merry; that is the best armour against love. What ruins women? Revery and sentimentality. A woman who does not laugh ought to be watched."

But though she lectured and advised Aspatria as to the ways of men and the ways of love, Sarah had not much faith in her own counsels. "No one can draw out a programme for a woman's happiness," she mused; "she will not keep to its lines. Now, I do wonder whether she will dress gorgeously or not? What did Solomon in all his glory wear? If Aspatria only knew how dress catches a man's eye, and then touches his vanity, and then sets fire to his imagination, and finally, somehow, someway, gets to his heart! If she only knew, —

' All thoughts, all passions, all delights,
  Whatever stirs this mortal frame,
Are but the ministers of Love,
  And feed his sacred flame ! ' "

A little before nine, Ulfar entered Sarah's
drawing-room. It was lighted with wax
candles. It was sweet with fresh violets,
and at the farther end Aspatria stood by
her harp. She was dressed for Lady
Chester's ball, and was waiting her chap-
eron ; but there had been a little rebellion
against her leaving without giving her
admirers one song. Every person was
suggesting his or her favourite ; and she
stood smiling, uncertain, listening, watching, for one voice and face.

Her dazzling bodice was clasped with
emeralds ; her draperies were of damasked
gauze, shot with gold and silver, and
abloom with flowers. Her fair neck spark-
led with diamonds ; and the long white
fingers which touched the strings so firmly
glinted with flashing gems. The moment
Ulfar entered, she saw him. His eyes, full
of fiery prescience, forced her to meet their
inquiry ; and then it was that she sat down

and filled the room with tinkling notes,
that made every one remember the mountains, and the merry racing of the spring
winds, and the trickling of half-hidden
fountains.

Sarah advanced with him. She touched
Aspatria slightly, and said: "Hush! a
moment. This is my friend Sir Ulfar
Fenwick, Ria."

Ria lifted her eyes sweetly to his eyes;
she bowed with the grace and benignity of
a queen, and adroitly avoided speech by
turning the melody into song: —

> "I never shall forget
> The mountain maid that once I met
> By the cold river's side.
> I met her on the mountain-side;
> She watched her herds unnoticed there:
> ' Trim-bodiced maiden, hail!' I cried.
> She answered, ' Whither, Wanderer?
> For thou hast lost thy way.'"

Every word went to Ulfar's heart, and
amid all the soft cries of delight he alone
was silent. She was beaming with smiles;
she was radiant as a goddess; the light
seemed to vanish from the room when she

went away. Her adieu was a general one,
excepting to Ulfar. On him she turned
her bright eyes, and courtesied low with
one upward glance. It set his heart on
fire. He knew that glance. They might
say this or that, they might lie to him
neck-deep, he knew it was Aspatria! He
was cross with Sarah. He accused her of
downright deception. He told her frankly
that he believed nothing about the soldier
and his sister.

She bade him come in the morning and
talk to Ria; and he asked impetuously:
" How soon? Twelve, I suppose? How
am I to pass the time until twelve
to-morrow?"

" Why this haste? "

" Why this deception? "

" After seven years' indifference, are you
suddenly gone mad? "

" I feel as if I was being very badly
used."

" How does the real Aspatria feel? Go
at once to Ambar-Side."

"The real Aspatria is here.   I know it! I feel it!"

"In a court of law, what evidence would feeling be?"

"In a court of love — "

"Try it."

"I will, to-morrow, at ten o'clock."

His impetuosity pleased her.   She was disposed to leave him to Aspatria now. And Aspatria was disposed on the following morning to make his confession very easy to him.   She dressed herself in the simple black gown she had kept ready for this event.   It had the short elbow sleeves, and the ruffle round the open throat, and the daffodil against her snowy breast, that distinguished the first costume he had ever seen her in.   She loosened her hair and let it fall in two long braids behind her ears.   She was, as far as dress could make her so, the Aspatria who had held the light to welcome him to Ambar-Side that stormy night ten years ago.

He was standing in the middle of the

room, restless and expectant, when she
opened the door. He called her by name,
and went to meet her. She trembled and
was silent.

"Aspatria, it is you! My Life! My
Soul! It is you!"

He took her hands; they were as cold
as ice. He drew her close to his side; he
stooped to see her eyes; he whispered word
upon word of affection, — sweet-meaning
nouns and adjectives that caught a real
physical heat from the impatient heart and
tongue that forged and uttered them.

"Forgive me, my dearest! Forgive me
fully! Forgive me at once and altogether!
Aspatria, I love you! I love none but
you! I will adore you all my life! Speak
one word to me, one word, my love, one
word: say only 'Ulfar!'"

She forgot in a moment all that she had
suffered. She forgot all she had promised
Sarah, all her intents of coldness, all re-
proaches; she forgot even to forgive him.
She just put her arms around his neck and

kissed him. She blotted out the past forever in that one whispered word, " Ulfar."

And then he took her to his heart; he kissed her for very wonder; he kissed her for very joy; but most of all he kissed her for fervent love. Then once more life was an " Interlude in Heaven." Every hour held some sweet surprise, some accidental joy. It was Brune, it was Sarah, it was some eulogium of Ulfar in the great London weeklies. He had fought in the good fight for freedom; he had done great deeds of mercy as well as of valour; he had crossed primeval forests, and brought back wonderful medicines, and dyes, and many new specimens for the botanist and the naturalist. The papers were never weary in praising his pluck, his bravery, his generosity, and his endurance; the Geographical Society sent him its coveted blue ribbon. In his own way Ulfar had made himself a fit mate for the new Aspatria.

And she was a constant wonder to him. Nothing in all his strange experience

touched his heart like the thought of his
simple, patient wife, studying to please
him, to be worthy of his love. Every day
revealed her in some new and charming
light. She was one hundred Aspatrias in
a single, lovable, lovely woman. On what,
ever subject Ulfar spoke, she understood,
supplemented, sympathized with, or assisted him. She could talk in French and
Italian; she was not ignorant of botany
and natural science, and she was delighted
to be his pupil.

In a single month they became all the
world to each other; and then they began
to long for the lonely old castle fronting
the wild North Sea, to plan for its restora-
tion, and for a sweet home-life, which
alone could satisfy the thirst of their
hearts for each other's presence. At the
end of June they went northward.

It was the month of the rose, and the
hedges were pink, and the garden was a
garden of roses. There were banks of
roses, mazes of roses, walks and standards

of roses, masses of glorious colour, and breezes scented with roses. Butterflies were chasing one another among the flowers; nightingales, languid with love, were singing softly above them. And in the midst was a gray old castle, flying its old border flags, and looking as happy as if it were at a festival.

Aspatria was enraptured, spellbound with delight. With Ulfar she wandered from one beauty to another, until they finally reached a great standard of pale-pink roses. Their loveliness was beyond compare; their scent went to the brain like some divine essence. It was a glory, — a prayer, — a song of joy! Aspatria stood beside it, and seemed to Ulfar but its mortal manifestation. She was clothed in a gown of pale-pink brocade, with a little mantle of the same, trimmed with white lace, and a bonnet of white lace and pink roses. She was a perfect rose of womanhood. She was the glory of his life, his prayer, his song of joy!

" It is the loveliest place in the world!"
he said, "and you! you are the loveliest
woman! My sweet Aspatria!"

She smiled divinely. "And yet," she
answered, " I remember, Ulfar, a song of
yours that said something very different.
Listen: —

> ' There is a rose of a hundred leaves,
> *But the wild rose is the sweetest!*' "

And as she sang the words, Ulfar had a
vision of a young girl, fresh and pure as a
mountain bluebell, in her scrimp black
frock. He saw the wind blowing it tight
over her virgin form; he saw her fair,
childish, troubled face as she kissed him
farewell in the vicar's meadows; and then
he saw the glorious woman, nobly planned,
perfect on every side, that the child wife
had grown to.

So, when she ceased, he pulled the fair-
est rose on the tree; he took from it every
thorn, he put it in her breast, he kissed
the rose, and he kissed her rose-like face.
Then he took up the song where she

dropped it; and hand in hand, keeping
time to its melody, they crossed the threshold of their blessed home.

" The robin sang beneath the eaves :
 ' There is a rose of a hundred leaves,
 But the wild rose is the sweetest !'

" The nightingale made answer clear :
 ' *O darling rose ! more fair, more dear !*
 O rose of a hundred leaves !' "

THE END.